INSIGHTS INTO ACADEMIC WRITING

INSIGHTS INTO ACADEMIC *Writing*

Strategies for Advanced Students

MARGOT C. KADESCH
ELLEN D. KOLBA
SHEILA C. CROWELL

Addison-Wesley Publishing Company
Reading, Massachusetts • Menlo Park, California
New York • Don Mills, Ontario • Wokingham, England
Amsterdam • Bonn • Sydney • Singapore • Tokyo
Madrid • San Juan • Paris • Seoul, Korea • Milan
Mexico City • Taipei, Taiwan

Insights into Academic Writing: Strategies for Advanced Students

Executive editor: Joanne Dresner
Development editor: Penny Laporte
Production editor: Janice L. Baillie
Text design: Pencil Point Studio
Cover design: Pencil Point Studio
Text art: Ray Skibinski

Library of Congress Cataloging in Publication Data

Kadesch, Margot C.
  Insights into academic writing: strategies for advanced students
/ by Margot C. Kadesch, Ellen D. Kolba, Sheila C. Crowell.
      p.   cm.
  ISBN 0-8013-0364-8
  1. English language – Rhetoric – Study and teaching.   2. English
language – Study and teaching – Foreign speakers.   I. Kolba, Ellen.
1940-   II. Crowell, Sheila C.   III. Title,
  PE1404.K34   1991
808'.042 – dc20   90-25667
                                                        CIP

7 8 9 10-CRS-99 98 97

To Bob, Marshall, and Caleb for their encouragement and support, and to the spirit of collaboration that made this book possible.

Contents

UNIT THREE
Summarizing and Reacting to What You Have Read   37

Philosophy
Topic: Moral Codes
Writing Assignment: Summarizing and Reacting to Readings

UNIT FOUR
Responding to Literature   53

Poetry
Topic: Analyzing Images in a Poem
Writing Assignment: A Critical Essay

UNIT FIVE
Taking Written Tests   73

Economics
Topic: Scarcity and Choice
Writing Assignment: Writing an Essay Test

UNIT SIX
Expressing an Opinion   89

Business
Topic: What Makes Work Satisfying
Writing Assignment: An Opinion Essay

UNIT SEVEN
Taking a Position   107

History, Law, and Political Science
Topic: First Amendment Rights
Writing Assignment: Taking and Supporting a Position

UNIT EIGHT
Writing a Term Paper, Part 1:
Developing a Thesis   123

 Technology
Topic: The Impact of Technology on the Workplace
Writing Assignment: Developing a Preliminary Thesis
Statement

UNIT NINE
Writing a Term Paper, Part 2:
Gathering and Organizing Information   134

Technology
Topic: The Impact of Technology on the Workplace
Writing Assignment: The First Draft of a Term Paper

UNIT TEN
Writing a Term Paper, Part 3:
Revising   155

Technology
Topic: The Impact of Technology on the Workplace
Writing Assignment: The Final Draft of a Term Paper

Acknowledgments

The authors would like to thank the following teachers and their students for trying out this book in all its stages of development, for giving us access to their classes and their essays, and for providing us with both encouragement and suggestions that contributed greatly to the final direction of the book: Joan Greenbaum, La Guardia Community College, City University of New York; Susan Gunter, Westminster College of Salt Lake City; Charlene Langfur, William Paterson College, Wayne, New Jersey; Alice Lyons-Quinn, Boston University, Center for English Language and Orientation Programs; and Carol Numrich, Columbia University, American Language Program.

In addition, the faculty of Westminster College of Salt Lake City and Joan Greenbaum of La Guardia Community College were helpful in suggesting texts and in discussing their expectations of student writing.

Special thanks are also owed to Joanne Dresner for her vision in putting the three of us together and to Penny Laporte, whose sense of language made being edited a pleasure.

To the Teacher

Insights into Academic Writing is an advanced writing course for native and non-native speakers of English enrolled in college-level writing classes. The course focuses on the academic writing tasks students must master if they are to succeed in college.

Every unit presents students with a writing assignment typical of those required in college courses—comparing events or attitudes, responding to literature, summarizing and reacting to texts, stating and supporting an opinion, and writing a logical argument. In addition, Unit Five both reviews the teaching points previously introduced and asks students to apply what they have learned to answering test questions. The last three units take students step by step through writing a controlled term paper for which all source materials are provided.

One of the features of this book is that students are expected to use the readings, prewriting exercises, and class discussions as source materials for their writing. The theory behind the organization of the units is that, before students can write an interesting and informative essay, they must think about the topic and deal with it in a variety of modes. Thus, students are asked to read about the topic, to do simple research or make observations to verify what they have learned, to report on and compare their findings with those of others in the class, and to perform formative writing tasks such as taking notes, summarizing, or writing definitions. After the first unit, which assigns a personal essay, the materials encourage exposition and support students in integrating what they know and have learned into thoughtful and analytical essays.

Every unit presents and practices two teaching points. The first one is presented before students write the first draft of their essays, and treats such global rhetorical issues as developing and supporting a thesis, structuring an essay, and organizing ideas. The second point, presented and practiced before students write the second draft, treats somewhat more localized rhetorical issues, such as moving from general to specific and from specific to general, developing topic sentences, organizing paragraphs, and using quotations for support.

Organization of the Units

The units are organized into the following sections:

Getting Ready to Write
- Prereading questions
- Reading selections followed by discussion questions
- A brief warm-up in which students begin to put their ideas down on paper
- Prewriting activities in which students verify and report on what they have learned from the reading

The First Draft
- Presentation of the first teaching point, followed by exercises
- The writing assignment, with instructions about content, target audience, and procedure

The Second Draft
- Presentation of the second teaching point, followed by exercises
- The revision assignment, with a checklist of points to which students should pay special attention

Each unit has been carefully designed to lead students through the writing process from the prewriting stage, in which they gather and verify information, to composing a first draft on the topic, to writing the second draft.

The last three units cover the term paper and operate as a single writing process. Unit Eight takes students through the prewriting activities, Unit Nine gets students ready to write and assigns the first draft, and Unit Ten supports students in writing the second draft.

The Reading Selections

The readings in this book are all drawn from college-level texts in the humanities, sciences, social sciences, and business. The selections serve two purposes: (1) to provide students with information about various topics and (2) to give them experience in getting information from college-level texts. The prereading exercises that precede the selections are designed to develop the concept formation necessary for understanding the selections. The discussion questions that follow are designed to foster comprehension and to encourage students to relate the information in the reading to their own experience.

Some students will find the vocabulary and sentence structure of the readings difficult. However, one of the objectives of this text is to accustom them to deriving information from materials they may find difficult—a skill they must master if they are to succeed in college. As a result, the readings should *not* be used to give students practice in intensive reading, nor should they be examined as models for the students' own writing. Instead, instructors should encourage students to get from the texts all the information they can and to relate what they have learned to what they already know and have experienced. The prereading and discussion questions support students to this end.

The Formative Writing Tasks

The materials in this book require students to complete many kinds of formative writing tasks before they ever sit down to compose a first draft. The prereading concept-formation activities often require them to complete sentences or write lists and definitions. Some questions in the discussion sections require note taking, while the writing warm-ups require students to react in writing to what they have read. Finally, the prewriting activities all require extensive note taking, often in the form of charts or lists in which students record their findings or outline their ideas.

Students should refer to their formative writing notes when they write their essays. A good way to help them keep their notes is to require that they be recorded in writing journals, which are collected and checked from time to time. It is not necessary to grade the journals; however, comments or suggestions in the margins may help students compose more effectively.

The Exercises

The exercises not only present the rhetorical structures and writing strategies students need in order to carry out the assignment, but most constitute formative writing activities as well. The content of the exercises is consistent with that of the units. As a result, students have yet another opportunity to put their ideas about the topic into words.

The exercises present and practice the teaching points step by step. They have been sequenced to take students from *recognition* to *application*. As a result, students first identify the target structure, then they produce it. Finally, they apply it to their own writing, either when they compose the first draft or when they write the second draft.

Responding to Students' Drafts

The best way to teach students to write is to read their papers holistically and provide both formative and summative evaluation. Evaluation of the first draft is done in two steps. The initial reading should be done quickly, without pencil in hand, to gain a general impression of the content. The instructor acts as an interested reader, noting what works, what is confusing, what seems incomplete, and what he or she would like to know more about. In the second step of the formative evaluation, the instructor reads the first draft as an editor, making suggestions about the development and organization of the content to help students revise.

Peer and small-group conferencing can be used as part of the formative evaluation. The advantages are twofold. Students are willing to listen to comments and suggestions from peers, particularly on issues of clarity and completeness. They are also able to see problems in the writing of others that they cannot identify in their own work and to transfer this insight to their own writing.

In order for peer conferencing to be successful, it first needs to be modeled in instructor-student conferences in the language of the comments the instructor writes on student papers. The procedure given as part of the first-draft assignment and the checklists for revision can be used as guidelines for peer and small-group conferences, as well as for self-evaluation.

While formative evaluation is often ungraded because its purpose is to help students in their revisions, the goal of summative evaluation is to provide a grade. Although students will not usually produce a third draft of a paper, the instructor should make general comments that will help students repeat what they have done successfully and become aware of areas that still need improvement.

Planning the Course

Most of the units in *Insights into Academic Writing* will take two weeks of class time to complete. In general, the activities leading to composition of the first draft will occupy the first week, while the second week will be devoted to presenting the second teaching point, allowing time for students to hold conferences on their first drafts in pairs or small groups, and for assigning the second draft.

Supporting students as they revise their writing is an integral part of this course. As a result, instructors are discouraged from omitting the section of each unit that presents the second teaching point and assigns the second draft. Instructors who are pressed for time might omit the last three units, which cover the term paper, or select only those units that introduce teaching points they feel their students need most urgently.

The following schedule is suggested for a sixteen-week semester:

Unit One	Week 1
Unit Two	Weeks 2 and 3
Unit Three	Weeks 4 and 5
Unit Four	Weeks 6 and 7
Unit Five	Week 8
Unit Six	Weeks 9 and 10
Unit Seven	Weeks 11 and 12
Unit Eight	Weeks 13 and 14
Unit Nine	Week 15
Unit Ten	Week 16

UNIT ONE
GETTING IDEAS FROM PERSONAL EXPERIENCE

Social Science

In this unit you are going to read two selections about what happens to people psychologically when they go to live in a foreign country. One of these selections describes the stages of adjustment people experience in a new setting. The other describes the actual experience of a traveler to a new country. The writing assignment will be to discuss something that surprised you when you visited or went to live in a new place.

GETTING READY TO WRITE

You will be reading about surprise and shock in this unit. The following activity uses the inquiry method to explore ideas related to these concepts.

Work in small groups to discuss the situations and answer the questions. Don't worry if you disagree with others in your group. The more you talk, the clearer your ideas will become.

1. When Juan and Antonia got married, Antonia's brother Paulo was there. Antonia had not seen Paulo in sixteen years.
   • How do you think Antonia felt?
   • How do you think Juan felt?

2. Paulo told his family that he had been in jail all that time.
   • How do you think Antonia felt?
   • How do you think Juan felt?

3. None of the wedding guests would talk to Paulo.
   • How do you feel about the wedding guests' behavior?

4. Paulo gave the newlyweds a check for $25,000.
   • How do you think Juan felt?
   • How do you think Antonia felt?

5. Paulo had been jailed wrongly, so the government gave him a huge sum of money as compensation.
   - How do you think Juan felt?
   - How do you think Antonia felt?
   - How do you think Paulo felt?
   - How do you feel about this information?

Now use the situations you have just discussed to define *surprise*. **Think about the kinds of events you have described as surprising. Also think about other words you have used to describe these events. Did you use any of the words and phrases below in your discussion?**

- shocked/terribly shocked
- pleasant/unpleasant
- unexpected/just what you'd expect

Can you use any of these words or phrases in your definition?

I. Adjusting to a New Culture or Place

In 1960 the anthropologist Kalervo Oberg was the first to use the term *culture shock* to describe the emotional difficulties of a newcomer in a foreign country. In this selection you will learn what Oberg meant by *culture shock*.

Before you read the first selection, "The Stages of Adjustment," think about a trip you have taken to another city or country. Then discuss the following questions with your classmates.

1. How did you feel before you left? What did you think about?

2. What new or different things did you observe when you arrived?

3. Did you miss any of the comforts of your home, such as your own bed, your favorite foods, or special ways of doing things? If so, how did missing them make you feel?

4. How did you feel after you returned home?

THE STAGES OF ADJUSTMENT

Someone who goes to stay in a foreign country, whether it is for a short time or forever, passes through several stages of adjusting to the newness of the culture. If the stay is going to be short, the person moves quickly through the stages. If the stay will be long, the stages last longer. Even children, who seem more adaptable than adults, go through the adjustment cycle, though they pass through it rather quickly.

The first stage of adjustment begins before the travelers even leave home. During this stage they form ideas and images of what life in the new country will be like. In a way, they imagine themselves into the new way of life. It is a way to begin adjusting to the change.

In the second stage, which begins when the travelers arrive in the new country, everything is new and interesting. The travelers are in a heightened state of emotion, and their moods swing wildly up and down. While they are intensely aware of everything around them, they have no framework into which to put what they see and smell and hear. All their impressions tend to run together, or merge. Travelers at this stage are passive. They watch the inhabitants of their new land, but they do not join in. They are merely spectators.

As the travelers spend more time in the new country, the second stage gradually gives way to the third, or participation, stage. During this stage, the travelers begin entering into the life of the new country. They are no longer spectators, but begin taking part. And as they participate, difficulties arise. They make mistakes; they find it difficult to accomplish simple tasks in a new country with an unfamiliar language and customs.

This is the stage where there is the most variability. Some travelers find it challenging. They learn from their mistakes and gradually begin to feel more a part of the country. Others find the task of adjusting nearly overwhelming. But even those who find it difficult gradually—almost against their will—begin participating more and more.

As the travelers participate more in the life of the new country, they begin changing. What was strange becomes familiar. What was difficult becomes easy. What seemed impossible becomes possible. Bit by bit they leave behind some of the assumptions and behaviors and beliefs which were part of them in their native land and begin thinking and acting more like the inhabitants of the new country. They have entered the fourth, or culture shock, stage of adjustment.

By the fourth stage the travelers are functioning well. The language is no longer the struggle it once was. The currency is no longer unfamiliar. They know what to expect and how to get what they want.

And just at this time a strange thing happens. They begin to feel more alienated than they did when they first arrived. Though life has become easier and they are coping well, they become irritable. Some become depressed. What they once found exciting and interesting in the new country is now annoying or hateful. They no longer want to go out and explore their new surroundings. They withdraw into themselves. They are experiencing the classic symptoms of culture shock.

What has happened is that by adjusting to their new surroundings, they have lost their sense of self. In giving up a little of their old culture and taking on some of the new, the very foundations of their identity are threatened. It is a frightening experience, and they cope with their fear by withdrawing from the new culture and temporarily retreating back to being spectators. Some even find that they can no longer use the new language as well as they had only days or weeks before.

This stage, the culture shock stage, may be long or short, depending on the individual. Eventually, though, the travelers begin participating again in the culture and they find to their amazement that they no longer feel so foreign. Out of the depression and sense of loss they experienced in the fourth stage comes real adjustment to the new land. They are less excited than they were in stage two, but their experiences are no longer a blur of heightened emotions and senses. They participate more than they did in stage three, but with less effort. In short, they have adapted to and become a part of their new country.

The final stage, the re-entry stage, occurs when or if the travelers return to their native lands. When they do, they find that they are not quite the same people as they were when they left. They have changed. Their values may be broader and more flexible. They have learned new and often better ways of being and thinking. Their friends and family seem slightly narrow and inflexible. Worse, their friends and family are only mildly interested in the exciting things that happened to them during their sojourn abroad. To their amazement, they feel just a little bit foreign in their own homeland.

Needless to say, personality differences influence the degree to which travelers go through these stages of adjustment. For some, the second stage is merely one of gentle interest in their new surroundings, while they experience culture shock only as a mild listlessness or lack of interest in what is going on. Others feel the full force of each stage, going from excitement to despair, fully aware of the imbalance they experience as one stage gives way to another. Nevertheless, all travelers go through these stages of adjustment to a greater or lesser degree, and none return to their homes as quite the same people who left.

THINK AND DISCUSS

Think about the following questions. Then discuss them with your classmates.

1. What are the stages of adjustment?

2. What happens to the traveler at each stage of adjustment?

3. When people are badly frightened or badly injured they go into shock. They are cold. They lose their ability to feel. Often they are not able to think clearly. Which stage of adjustment is called *culture shock*? Why do you think Oberg chose the word *shock* to name this stage of adjustment?

4. Why do you think returning home is listed as one of the stages of adjustment? Why would a person have to adjust to living again in his or her own country?

5. Think about the trip you discussed before you read "The Stages of Adjustment." Did you go through any of these stages? If so, which ones? How were your reactions at each stage similar to or different from those described in the reading selection?

Think about what it means to be adjusted to a new situation, such as a new school, a new city, or a new country. Write some words and phrases you associate with adjusting to something new.

_____

_____

_____

_____

II. Adjusting to New Customs and Routines

The next selection was written by Margot C. Kadesch, one of the authors of this book. In it, she describes her own experience with culture shock when she spent a year in Yugoslavia in 1981.

Before you read, do the following activity to help you examine how you feel when your customs and routines are disrupted.

Think about things that you do nearly every day and complete the statements below.

I am accustomed to . . .

I usually . . .

I always . . .

Now think about how you feel when you aren't able to do or have the things you are accustomed to, such as eating at your usual time, being treated in the way you expect, or understanding how to do something. Then complete the statements below.

When I can't _____ I feel . . .

If I don't _____ I . . .

It makes me feel _____ when _____ don't/doesn't . . .

IT'S IN THE BAG

I don't know what I expected when I went to live in Yugoslavia for a year, but I certainly didn't expect that every man, woman, and child I saw would be carrying a plastic bag. Before I left, I spent quite a bit of time imagining what my life there would be like and wondering what the people would be like. I fantasized about fiery Serbs and rugged Croats. I pictured a simple people, cut off from the West and not at all like Europeans from, say, nearby Italy or Germany.

I really didn't know much about Yugoslavia before I went there. I had a vague picture of it as a misty, romantic place where the peasants wore colorful embroidered clothes and the folk arts flourished. I had heard of Tito, of course, and knew that Yugoslavia had a communistic form of government. In addition, I had been studying the language and had a few handy phrases on the tip of my tongue. I had also read a little about the history of Yugoslavia, which contributed to my vision of a misty, romantic country where the peasants wore colorful clothes . . . etc.

The reality was quite different from what I had imagined, while at the same time it was quite a bit *like* what I had imagined. In some regions of the country the peasants do wear colorful and beautifully embroidered clothes, especially for festivals. And the folk arts—not to mention the modern arts—do indeed flourish. Tito *was* a major force in Yugoslavia and the government is undeniably communistic. It was this latter bit of information that left me so unprepared for all those plastic bags.

I pictured a communist country as a place where gray-faced people shuffled along in drab clothing and stood in endless lines for dark bread and a handful of potatoes. I imagined oppression and shortages. I expected to live a life of privation in Yugoslavia, quite unlike the comfortable life I lived in America.

The Yugoslavs turned out to be neither gray-faced, oppressed, nor standing in bread lines. They are lusty, handsome, freedom-loving people and are more apt to be found lounging in a *kavana* (a local coffee house) than standing in a bread line.

In fact, the shops were stocked with consumer goods, and food was both plentiful and delicious. Everyone had a television set and many had electric washing machines. Freezers were new on the market and were the current rage, and everywhere you looked people were shopping for the good things of life.

So that's why they all carried bags.

Shops in Yugoslavia do not bag your purchases as they do in the United States. Instead, you are handed your bread naked. You supply the bag when you buy potatoes. Eggs don't come in egg cartons. The shopkeeper places them in your bag unwrapped, one by one—on top of the green beans and bread and laundry soap. As a result, every housewife stows at least one—and more likely two—bags in her handbag for shopping on the way home from work. Men tuck bags in their pockets or carry them like briefcases, with the morning paper and an umbrella inside.

Even children carry plastic bags. Girls use them to carry girl things. Boys stuff them with boy things. And children routinely act as porters for their mothers on shopping trips. Toddlers are started out with small plastic training bags. They hold their mothers' hands with one hand and in the other clutch the ubiquitous plastic bag, complete with bottle, blanket, and favorite toy.

One thing that puzzled me was how to get started in the bag game. I needed bags to do my shopping, but they weren't for sale in any of the stores. And they certainly weren't given out in the grocery stores. I spent a miserable few days buying only as much food at one time as I could carry in my hands and put in my pockets. This meant that I had to make several shopping trips a day just to keep myself fed. I couldn't imagine where people *got* their bags, though in the hand of every citizen hurrying along the crowded streets was ample evidence that bags existed.

Finally a kind woman at a checkout stand came to my rescue. I had bought more groceries than I intended and, as the clerk rang up my purchases, I wondered how on earth I would get them home without a bag. The clerk gave me the receipt and then asked me something in rapid Serbo-Croatian. I couldn't understand a word. So she repeated her question louder and still more rapidly. I shook my head and tried to stuff the groceries in my pockets. Then the clerk really yelled. I wanted to tell her that I wasn't deaf; I just didn't understand the language very well. She kept pointing at my purchases and my wallet.

I was totally bewildered. Surely I had paid in full for my groceries. Nevertheless, I opened my wallet. To my surprise, the woman behind me in line reached in it, took out two dinar coins, and slapped them down in front of the irate clerk. Quick as a wink, the clerk reached under the counter and brought out a brand new, beautiful plastic bag. It was mine. All mine!

I will always think of that unknown woman as my personal fairy godmother. From then on, shopping was in the bag. It took me several months to learn the proper words, but I could always get a new bag any time I wanted by slapping two dinars down and pointing under the counter. In no time at all I had a lovely supply. The extras hung on a hook in my kitchen, and two were always nestled in my handbag at the ready. Soon I was just another woman carrying a plastic bag along the cobbled streets of Yugoslavia.

THINK AND DISCUSS

Think about the following questions. Then discuss them with your classmates.

1. What did Ms. Kadesch assume about life in Yugoslavia? Was she right? Why or why not?

2. What was Ms. Kadesch accustomed to when she bought groceries?

3. What was the Yugoslav custom?

4. Why was Ms. Kadesch surprised to see everyone carrying plastic bags? What were her assumptions?

5. How do you think small things, such as not knowing how to get a shopping bag, contribute to culture shock?

6. From what you learned about the stages of adjustment, what stage do you think the writer was in when she
   • imagined what life in Yugoslavia would be like?
   • first noticed all the people carrying shopping bags?
   • described herself as "just another woman carrying a plastic bag along the cobbled streets of Yugoslavia"?

7. When you go to a new country or a new place, things often seem different, strange, or even foreign. We often use the words *new*, *different*, *strange*, and *foreign* and expressions that are related to them without being conscious of our feelings about them. For example, what are your feelings about the word *stranger*? Are they positive or negative? Discuss with your classmates your feelings about the expressions below.

newcomer	a new experience	a new way of doing things
being different	different customs	different from us
looking strange	strange food	stranger
foreign currency	foreign accent	foreigner

WRITING WARM-UP

Think about new experiences you have had in which you felt surprised, strange, or foreign. List some of the words and phrases that come to mind when you recall the incidents.

_____

_____

_____

_____

THE FIRST DRAFT
Learning about Writing I

You have read about culture shock and about what surprised one person when she visited a new place. Before you start writing about your own experience, you need to understand something about the writing process.

Read the section "What Is the Writing Process?" and answer the questions. Then do the prewriting exercises. You will learn some techniques that will help you get started and help you focus your ideas when you write.

WHAT IS THE WRITING PROCESS?

Writing involves more than just putting words down on paper. Before writers sit down with a pen, typewriter, or word processor, they think about the topic or gather information about it. Then they write. But the writing process doesn't end when a writer finishes his or her first try. Most writers write and rewrite several times before they feel satisfied with what they have said. We call this process of thinking and gathering information, writing, and rewriting, the writing process. The writing process is usually divided into three steps: prewriting, drafting, and revising.

Prewriting.   Prewriting is the first stage of writing. It includes reading, discussing, and thinking about the topic in a variety of ways, such as doing research and taking notes, making lists, and developing outlines. It even includes unconscious processes in which your mind works on the topic even though you are not consciously thinking about it. During the prewriting stage, you focus your ideas and begin to organize them.

You have already done some prewriting for your essay by reading about adjusting to a new culture. What other kinds of prewriting have you done?

Drafting.   Drafting is actually writing your essay. In order to write a good essay, you need to write more than one draft. In your first draft, you get your ideas down on paper in complete sentences and paragraphs. Then you can read what you have written and decide how to make your essay better. You can also ask others to read your essay and suggest how to improve it.

In this book, you will write only a first and a second draft of each essay; however, good writers often write three or more drafts in order to make their ideas perfectly clear to their readers.

Think about writing you have done in the past. Have you ever made more than one draft? If so, how many drafts did you make before you felt satisfied?

Revising.   Making changes in a draft to improve it is called *revising.* When you revise, you take out ideas, add ideas, rearrange ideas, or combine ideas.

If you have ever revised what you wrote, what kinds of changes did you make?

The three steps in the writing process will not always come one after the other in a neat order. While you are writing a draft, for example, you might change your mind about something and revise one or more paragraphs, even though you have not completed the draft. When you are revising, you may want to go back to the first step—prewriting—for new ideas or new ways of organizing your thoughts.

Editing.   There is a final step that is very important: *editing.* Editing is not really part of the writing process, but it is important to edit what you write before you hand it in or make it public in any way. When you edit, you correct spelling, usage, and punctuation.

PREWRITING

Prewriting takes many forms and has several purposes. The prewriting exercises in this book are designed to help you narrow your topic, get ideas, or organize your ideas. The following exercises will introduce you to some useful prewriting techniques. Do them all to find the ones that work best for you.

Exercise 1: Brainstorming

Brainstorming brings unconscious ideas and feelings to the surface. You can use brainstorming to help you decide what to write about or to develop specific details after you have chosen a topic. Follow the steps below to practice brainstorming.

1. Set a timer for five minutes or have someone time you.

2. Think about new places you have visited and new experiences you have had.

3. On a sheet of paper, list everything you think of. Write words or short phrases, not sentences. Some of the things you list might name new experiences. Some might describe your feelings or describe what happened. Write down everything you think of, even if it seems unimportant.

4. Read over your list. Does it give you any new ideas about new places or experiences?

5. Save your list. You will use it later.

Exercise 2: Freewriting

In freewriting, you choose a topic and write about it for several minutes without stopping. Like brainstorming, freewriting helps you get your ideas flowing. Freewriting, however, is different from brainstorming because you write sentences in a paragraph instead of words or phrases in a list. Follow the steps below to practice freewriting.

1. Choose anything from the list you made when you brainstormed.

2. Set a timer for five minutes or have someone time you.

3. Write about the topic you chose. Don't worry about grammar or spelling or what word to use. Just keep writing whatever comes into your mind. If you get stuck, write the last word on your page over and over, or write something like "I don't know what to say next," until a new thought or idea comes to mind.

4. Keep writing until the time is up.

5. Save what you wrote. You will use it later.

Exercise 3: Visualizing

Visualizing helps you re-create things you have experienced or observed. It is an excellent way to gather concrete details that will make your reader understand your topic. When you visualize, you close your eyes and try to "relive" the experience. What did you "see," "hear," "smell," and "feel"? Follow the steps below to practice visualizing.

1. Work with a partner.

2. Close your eyes and visualize a place you know well. Focus on details: What kind of place is it? What do you see? How do you feel? What do you smell and hear? If other people are there, what do they look like? What do they do and say? What is happening? Did you visualize anything else that is unusual or interesting?

3. Tell your partner what you visualized. Try to describe it as concretely as possible so your partner can relive the experience with you.

4. Now let your partner tell you what he or she visualized.

5. Finally, choose a topic from the list you made while brainstorming. It can be the same topic you chose for freewriting or a new one. Repeat steps 2, 3, and 4 with the new topic.

Exercise 4: Questions

Asking questions can help you focus on a topic when you are not sure how to begin. It is also a good way to start thinking about your topic in a complete and thorough way. Follow the steps below to practice asking questions.

1. Choose a topic from your brainstorming list.

2. Use each of these question words to write a question about the topic you have chosen:

   Who . . .
   What . . .
   Where . .
   When . . .
   Why . . .

3. Now write brief answers to the questions. Your answers do not need to be complete sentences; a word or phrase will do.

4. Save your questions and answers. You will use them later.

Exercise 5: Grouping

Grouping is a technique that helps you make connections between ideas. It is a good technique to use for organizing your ideas after you have selected and thought about a topic. When grouping, a kind of map is drawn that shows how ideas and details are related. Here is an example of the way one student grouped her ideas when she thought about a visit to her friend Anna's house.

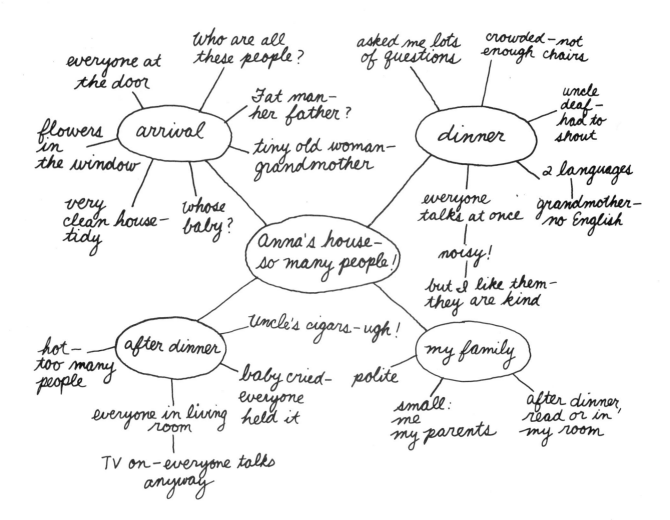

This student was surprised that Anna's family was so different from hers. When she did the prewriting exercise, she used visualizing to help her relive the experience. Then she grouped the differences she noticed into three situations: her arrival, dinner, and after dinner. Notice that she used a mixture of words, phrases, and sentences in this exercise. She also made a group of some ways in which her family was different from Anna's. She drew lines to connect the details to the appropriate group. Follow the steps below to practice grouping.

1. Choose a topic from your brainstorming list.

2. Write the topic in the center of a piece of paper.

3. Think about the topic and group your ideas on the paper. Include everything that occurs to you, even if it doesn't seem important. If you are not sure where something belongs, write it at the bottom or the side of your paper. Later you may see where it belongs or you may decide not to use it.

4. Now draw lines between details that belong together.

5. Spend about five minutes on this activity.

6. Save the paper on which you grouped your ideas. You will use it later.

Writing the First Draft

CONTENT

Write the first draft of an essay. In it, discuss what surprised you when you first went to a new place such as a new school, the home of a friend, another city, or a foreign country. What surprised you might be the appearance of the place, the way people looked or acted, or a custom such as the way a holiday was celebrated or how guests behaved at a party.

AUDIENCE

A writer's audience is the people who will read what the writer wrote. Your audience for this essay will be your instructor and the other students in the class. Before you revise, you will exchange papers with another student in the class who will read your essay and suggest ways to improve it. Keep this in mind as you write. Tell your audience what surprised you and describe exactly how and why you were surprised.

PROCEDURE

- Decide what new place you want to write about and what surprised you most when you went there. Choose one thing that surprised you; do not write about all the things that were surprising. Use the list you made when you brainstormed to help you.
- Select details that will help your readers understand your surprise. Use the readings, your notes from class discussions, writing warm-ups, and pre-writing exercises to help you select details. You may need to repeat one or more prewriting exercises now that you have decided on your topic.
- Use grouping to organize your details.
- Decide which group to write about first, which should be second, which should be third, and so on.
- Write your essay. It should be one to two double-spaced, typed pages or two to three double-spaced handwritten pages.

THE SECOND DRAFT

After you write a first draft, it is a good idea to put it away for a day or so before you revise it. Doing so allows you to look at your draft with a fresh eye and decide what needs to be changed.

Learning about Writing II

UNITY

There are certain characteristics that all good writing has. One of these is unity. In a unified piece of writing there is one main idea. Everything is related to the main idea: each sentence gives more information about, describes, or gives examples of the main idea. The exercises below will help you understand what unity is and how to unify your own writing. Do them before you revise your essay.

Exercise 1: Getting Rid of Sentences That Are Not Related

A. Each paragraph below has one sentence that destroys the unity of the paragraph. Find the sentence that is not related to the main idea and cross it out.

1. I never saw so many people intent on winning money until I went to Atlantic City. Everywhere I looked, there were people concentrating—on roulette wheels, on dice, on cards, on slot machines. Gambling is a serious addiction and should be treated like alcoholism. An earthquake could hit Atlantic City, and the people there would not move. They wouldn't want to miss a chance to win.

2. Everything around Paula seemed both completely familiar and totally foreign. She was in a park, seated on a bench, but the bench was a different shape and color from the benches at home. She was used to seeing flowers, shrubs, and trees growing in a park, but she was not used to seeing them planted in tubs the way they were here. At home, she walked to work every day, even in bad weather.

B. Compare your paragraphs with your classmates' and discuss why you crossed out particular sentences.

Exercise 2: Creating a Unified Paragraph

A. The first sentence in each group below expresses a main idea and is followed by a list of sentences. Use the main idea and sentences from the list to create a unified paragraph.

Use the main idea as the first sentence of the paragraph. Then arrange the sentences in the order you think best. (There is more than one way to do this.) Leave out any sentences that do not relate to the main idea.

1. Roberto was not prepared for the way New Yorkers ignored him.
   a. He expected to be welcomed warmly.
   b. He had heard that Los Angeles was a difficult city to get around in.
   c. He hadn't realized that New York was full of foreign visitors.
   d. No one seemed to notice him.
   e. He planned to stay for six months.
   f. For most New Yorkers, he was just like everyone else—another confused rider on the subway.

2. The hardest thing I ever had to do was change schools when I was eight years old.
   a. Writers often like to tell stories about their childhood.

b. Not only did I have a new teacher and new classmates, but I had to learn a whole new way of doing things.

c. I have had many new experiences since then.

d. Instead of using reading books, we went to the library.

e. We sat on the floor instead of at desks.

f. I never knew what to expect next.

B. Compare your paragraphs with your classmates' and discuss why the sentences you took out did not belong.

Exercise 3: Creating a Unified Essay

In Exercises 1 and 2 you practiced unifying paragraphs. Essays must also be unified. The main idea of an essay is often stated at the beginning and is developed in several paragraphs. The main idea of each paragraph must be related to the main idea of the essay. The details in each paragraph must be related to the main idea of the paragraph.

Read the main idea of an essay outlined below. Then read the main idea of each paragraph of that essay. Next, read the sentences on page 16 and decide which sentences belong in each paragraph. Every sentence in a paragraph should be related to the main idea of that paragraph. Arrange the sentences within each paragraph in the order that makes the most sense to you. Notice that some of the sentences on page 16 do not belong to this essay at all.

Main Idea of Essay

It's a mistake to think that knowing the language is all you need in order to get along in another country.

Main Idea of Paragraph 1

I went to France for the first time armed with words for every possible occasion.

Related Sentences

_____

_____

_____

Main Idea of Paragraph 2

However, nothing in my vocabulary helped me understand the strange customs of the Parisians.

Related Sentences

_____

_____

_____

Main Idea of Paragraph 3

I could have used a complete course in my adopted culture.

Related Sentences

_____

_____

_____

Choice of Related Sentences

- I didn't know that I would have to decide whether I was traveling first class or second class when I wanted to ride the metro.
- Then I would have felt comfortable with both the words and the actions of the Parisians.
- French was a much more difficult language for me to learn than Spanish.
- I could tell someone I liked the color of his eyes or ask him to stop bothering me.
- Most of all, I didn't know that new acquaintances would never invite me to their homes for dinner.
- Someone could have explained to me ahead of time that there was no point in going to the bakery between 2:00 and 4:00 P.M. because it would be closed.
- My favorite foods turned out to be omelettes and all kinds of French pastries.
- I could order food in a restaurant, ask to have a flat tire repaired, or report a theft to the police.
- I could have been told that I would never find hot oatmeal for breakfast or lined paper for my notebook.
- I didn't know that salad would be served at the end of the meal, not at the start.
- I took along nearly every French book I owned, including two dictionaries and a grammar book.
- I could even discuss the meaning of an obscure poem.
- Most of all they should have told me that the French are slower about considering you a friend than we are in America.

Exercise 4: Unifying Your Own Essay

Now identify the main ideas and supporting sentences in your first draft as you did in Exercise 3.

1. On the first line, write *Main Idea* and your main idea. You do not need to write complete sentences. Just write enough to remind you what your main idea is.

2. Write *Main Idea of Paragraph 1*, then write the main idea.

3. Write *Related Sentences*, then write the sentences that belong in this paragraph.

4. Do the same for the other paragraphs in your draft.

5. Read your outline critically to see if it is unified. Answer the following questions:
   - Did you write about only *one* thing that surprised you?
   - Is the main idea of each paragraph related to the main idea of the essay?
   - Are all the paragraphs unified? Are there any sentences that don't belong?

6. List the changes you plan to make when you revise your first draft.

Writing the Second Draft

Now it is time to revise your first draft. Exchange drafts with a partner and read each other's drafts. Using the questions below, suggest changes to make your partner's draft better. Add your partner's comments about your essay to the list of changes you made in Exercise 4 above.

- Is the essay unified? Is there one main idea? Is everything in the essay related to the main idea? Does each paragraph have a main idea? Are there any ideas that don't belong?
- Can you understand why the writer was surprised? Do the details let you share and relive the writer's experience?
- Are there any statements which you don't understand?
- Is there anything more you would like to know?

Now reread your own draft and decide what else you need to do in order to make your essay better. You may need to move things, add things, combine things, or take things out.

Writing the Final Copy

When you are finished revising, edit your essay for errors in spelling, grammar, and punctuation. If you have not already given your essay a title, add one now. Copy your revised draft neatly on clean paper before you hand it in to your instructor.

UNIT TWO
GETTING IDEAS FROM OBSERVATION

Anthropology

In this unit you are going to read two selections about the problems that arise when people from different cultures work together or socialize. One of these selections discusses the concept of time. The other discusses the concept of space. Both explore the variety of ways in which people deal with these two concepts.

In Unit One you described your own feelings about a new place. In this unit you will be observing and describing the feelings of others as they react to new cultures. Your writing assignment will be to compare and contrast the way in which two people behave with regard to time and space.

GETTING READY TO WRITE

I. The Silent Language of Time

Edward Hall, a noted anthropologist, wrote a book entitled *The Silent Language*. In this selection, you will learn what Hall means by the "silent language of time."

Before you read the first selection, "How Late Is Late?"
discuss the following situations.

1. You have an appointment with a very important person who has promised to help you. Your appointment is supposed to last one hour, but the important person ends the meeting after only fifteen minutes. How do you feel?

2. You invite a friend to dinner at 7:00 P.M. Your friend arrives at ten minutes after seven. Is your friend late? Should your friend apologize? What if your friend arrives at 7:35? At 8:00?

3. You have a business appointment at 2:00 P.M. You arrive at 2:00, but the person with whom you have the appointment keeps you waiting until 2:30. How do you feel? Do you think the person should apologize?

4. Someone else's idea of being late may be different from your own. Why is it important to be aware of this difference?

Vocabulary test #2

HOW LATE IS LATE?

Time talks. It speaks more plainly than words. The message it conveys comes through loud and clear. Because it is manipulated less consciously, it is subject to less distortion than the spoken language. It can shout the truth where words lie.

I was once a member of a mayor's committee on human relations in a large city. My assignment was to estimate what the chances were of non-discriminatory practices being adopted by the different city departments. The first step in this project was to interview the department heads, two of whom were themselves members of minority groups. If one were to believe the words of these officials, it seemed that all of them were more than willing to adopt non-discriminatory labor practices. Yet I felt that, despite what they said, in only one case was there much chance for a change. Why? The answer lay in how they used the silent language of time and space.

Special attention had been given to arranging each interview. Department heads were asked to be prepared to spend an hour or more discussing their thoughts with me. Nevertheless, appointments were forgotten; long waits in outer offices (fifteen to forty-five minutes) were common, and the length of the interview was cut often down to ten or fifteen minutes. I was usually kept at an impersonal distance during the interview. In only one case did the department head come from behind his desk. These men had a position, and they were literally and figuratively sticking to it!

The implication of this experience (one which public-opinion pollsters might well heed) is quite obvious. What people do is frequently more important than what they say. In this case the way these municipal potentates handled time was eloquent testimony to what they inwardly believed, for the structure and meaning of time systems, as well as the time intervals, are easy to identify. In regard to being late there are: "mumble something" periods, slight apology periods, mildly insulting periods requiring full apology, rude periods, and downright insulting periods.
. . .

Informally, for important daytime business appointments in the eastern United States between equals, there are eight time sets in regard to punctuality and length of appointments: on time, five, ten, fifteen, twenty, thirty, forty-five minutes, and one hour early or late. Keeping in mind that situations vary, there is a slightly different

Excerpts from The Silent Language *by Edward T. Hall, copyright © 1959 by Edward T. Hall. Used by permission of Doubleday, a division of Bantam, Doubleday, Dell Publishing Group, Inc.*

behavior pattern for each point, and each point on the scale has a different meaning. As for the length of appointments, an hour with an important person is different from thirty minutes with that same person. Ponder the significance of the remark, "We spent over an hour closeted with the President." Everyone knows the business must have been important. Or consider, "He could only spare ten minutes, so we didn't get much accomplished." Time then becomes a message as eloquently direct as if words were used. As for punctuality, no right-minded American would think of keeping a business associate waiting for an hour; it would be too insulting. No matter what is said in apology, there is little that can remove the impact of an hour's heel-cooling in an outer office.

Even the five-minute period has its significant subdivisions. When equals meet, one will generally be aware of being two minutes early or late but will say nothing, since the time in this case is not significant. At three minutes a person will still not apologize or feel that it is necessary to say anything (three is the first significant number in the one-to-five series); at five minutes there is usually a short apology; and at four minutes before or after the hour the person will mutter something, although he will seldom complete the muttered sentence. The importance of making detailed observations on these aspects of informal culture is driven home if one pictures an actual situation. An American ambassador in an unnamed country interpreted incorrectly the significance of time as it was used in visits by local diplomats. An hour's tardiness in their system is equivalent to five minutes by ours, fifty to fifty-five minutes to four minutes, forty-five minutes to three minutes, and so on for daytime official visits. By their standards the local diplomats felt they couldn't arrive exactly on time; this punctuality might be interpreted locally as an act relinquishing their freedom of action to the United States. But they didn't want to be insulting—an hour late would be too late—so they arrived fifty minutes late. As a consequence the ambassador said, "How can you depend on these people when they arrive an hour late for an appointment and then just mutter something? They don't even give you a full sentence of apology!" He couldn't help feeling this way, because in American time fifty to fifty-five minutes late is the insult period, at the extreme end of the duration scale; yet in the country we are speaking of it's just right.

THINK AND DISCUSS

Think about the following questions. Then discuss them with your classmates.

1. What were the department heads telling Hall by keeping him waiting and then not meeting for the full hour?

2. In the reading, Hall breaks lateness into five time periods. What are the names he gives to these periods? Why do you think Hall names the time periods in this way?

3. What is your own idea of lateness? If you had a business appointment, how many minutes late could you be before you felt the need to "mumble something," to make a slight apology, and so on?

4. Would your idea of lateness be different if you were going to a party instead of a business appointment? If so, describe the difference.

5. How would the following factors affect your idea of lateness for both business and social appointments?

- where you were meeting
- whether the person you were meeting was the same age as you
- whether the person you were meeting was your equal (socially or in business)
- how well you knew the person you were meeting

6. Compare your answers to questions 3, 4, and 5 with those of your classmates. Do people who come from the same country react in the same way? How are their answers the same? How are they different?

WRITING WARM-UP

Lateness is a concept. That is, it is an idea and not a thing that can be seen or touched or measured exactly. This activity will help you explore your own concept of lateness so you can be more precise in the way you talk and write about it.

List some ideas or special features you associate with the word *late*. Use any of the prewriting techniques you practiced in Unit One to help you get ideas. You do not need to write full sentences. Save your list. You will use it later.

_____

_____

_____

_____

II. The Silent Language of Space

People like to maintain a certain amount of distance between themselves and others when they interact in social or business situations. Anthropologists refer to this distance as *interaction distance*. In the selection that follows, Edward Hall describes cultural differences in interaction distance.

Before you read, discuss the following questions.

1. When someone stands too close to you, does it make you uncomfortable? What do you do to feel more comfortable?

2. When someone stands too far away from you, how do you feel? What do you do about it?

3. When you think about interacting with others, what words or feelings do you associate with "space," with "too close," and with "distant"?

HOW SPACE COMMUNICATES: INTERACTION DISTANCE

Vocabulary test #2

Spatial changes give a tone to a communication, accent it, and at times even override the spoken word. The flow and shift of distance between people as they interact with each other is part and parcel of the communication process. The normal conversational distance between strangers illustrates how important are the dynamics of space interaction. If a person gets too close, the reaction is instantaneous and automatic—the other person backs up. And if he gets too close again, back we go again. I have observed an American backing up the entire length of a long corridor while a foreigner whom he considers pushy tries to catch up with him. This scene has been enacted thousands and thousands of times—one person trying to increase the distance in order to be at ease, while the other tries to decrease it for the same reason, neither one being aware of what was going on. We have here an example of the tremendous depth to which culture can condition behavior.

One thing that does confuse us and gets in the way of understanding cultural differences is that there are times in our own culture when people are either distant or pushy in their use of space. We, therefore, simply associate the foreigner with the familiar; namely those people who have acted in such a way that our attention was drawn to their actions. The error is in jumping to the conclusion that the foreigner feels the same way the American does even though his overt acts are identical. This was suddenly brought into focus one time when I had the good fortune to be visited by a very distinguished and learned man who had been for many years a top-ranking diplomat representing a foreign country. After meeting him a number of times, I had become impressed with his extraordinary sensitivity to the small details of behavior that are so significant in the interaction process. Dr. X was interested in some of the work several of us were doing at the time and asked permission to attend one of my lectures. He came to the front of the class at the end of the lecture to talk over a number of points made in the preceding hour. While talking he became quite involved in the implications of the lecture as well as what he was saying. We started out facing each other and as he talked I became dimly aware that he was standing a little too close and that I was beginning to back up. Fortunately I was able to suppress my first impulse and remain stationary because there was nothing to communicate aggression in his behavior except the conversational distance. His voice was eager, his manner intent, the set of his body communicated only interest and eagerness to talk. It also came in a flash that someone who had been so successful in the old school of diplomacy could not possibly let himself communicate something offensive to the other person except outside of his highly trained awareness.

By experimenting I was able to observe that as I moved away slightly, there was an associated shift in the pattern of interaction. He had more trouble expressing himself. If I shifted to where I felt comfortable (about twenty-one inches), he looked somewhat puzzled and hurt, almost as though he were saying: "Why is he acting that way? Here I am doing everything I can to talk to him in a friendly manner and he suddenly withdraws. Have I done something wrong? Said something that I shouldn't?" Having ascertained that distance had a direct effect on his conversation, I stood my ground, letting him set the distance.

. . .

In Latin America the interaction distance is much less than it is in the United States. Indeed, people cannot talk comfortably with one another unless they are very close to the distance that evokes either sexual or hostile feelings in the North American. As a consequence, they think we are distant or cold, withdrawn and unfriendly. We, on the other hand, are constantly accusing them of breathing down our necks, crowding us, and spraying our faces.

THINK AND DISCUSS

Do the following activities. Then compare your observations with those of your classmates. How are they the same? How are they different? Do people who come from the same country or ethnic background react in the same way?

1. Why did Dr. X keep moving closer to Edward Hall when Hall stepped backward? To help you understand the scene with Hall and Dr. X, have two students go to the front of the class and act out what happened.

2. Work with a partner and begin talking about the weather, school, food, sports, or anything that comes into your head. As you talk, keep moving closer to your partner until the distance becomes uncomfortable for you. Your partner should stand still while you move. How close can you get before you cannot talk comfortably? Switch and let your partner try the same experiment.

3. Now start talking again, but this time keep moving away from your partner. Remember that your partner should stand still. How do you feel as the distance between you increases? At what point do you feel that you need to speak more loudly? At what distance do you become so uncomfortable that you want to stop talking? Switch and let your partner try the same experiment.

4. How do the following factors affect the way you feel about interaction distance?

   • whether the person you are talking to is male or female
   • whether the person you are talking to is the same age as you
   • how well you know the person you are talking to

5. When someone seems to come too close to you or to stand too far away, do you always interpret his or her actions accurately? Now that you have read Hall, do you think it is possible that your interaction distances are different?

WRITING WARM-UP

To help you be more precise when you discuss the concept of interaction distance, list some ideas or words you associate with the term. You do not need to write full sentences. Keep your list. You will use it later.

_____

_____

_____

_____

PREWRITING

In order to write the comparison-contrast essay assigned later in this unit, you will need to gather more information about how others handle time or space. The prewriting activities below will help you collect enough additional details to make an interesting essay. In the process of reading the two selections and completing the "Think and Discuss" activities, you may have decided which topic—time or space—you want to write about. If so, do just the activity that relates to your topic. If you haven't yet chosen a topic, doing both activities will help you decide.

TIME

Choose two people with different backgrounds and ask them the following questions about time. Make a chart like the one on page 26 for each person, and use it to record the answers. Ask what country each person is from or what ethnic group each one belongs to and record that information under the heading "background."

1. If you are expecting someone and he or she is late, after how many minutes do you feel that person should mutter a quick apology?

   • for a business meeting

   • for a social occasion

   How do you feel when someone has kept you waiting for this period of time? What do you do or say?

2. When should he or she make a slightly longer apology?

   • for a business meeting

   • for a social occasion

   How do you feel when someone has kept you waiting for this period of time? What do you do or say?

3. When should he or she make a full apology?

- for a business meeting
- for a social occasion

How do you feel when someone has kept you waiting for this period of time? What do you do or say?

4. After how many minutes do you begin to feel that he or she has been rude?

- for a business meeting
- for a social occasion

How do you feel when someone has kept you waiting for this period of time? What do you do or say?

5. After how many minutes do you think the person's behavior is insulting?

- for a business meeting
- for a social occasion

How do you feel when someone has kept you waiting for this period of time? What do you do or say?

	Name of Person: Background:	
	business meeting	social occasion
"mumble" something		
your feelings and reactions		
slight apology		
your feelings and reactions		
full apology		
your feelings and reactions		
rude		
your feelings and reactions		
downright insulting		
your feelings and reactions		

SPACE

**Observe several people in conversations outside of class.
Watch and listen to them. Take notes on what happens as
they talk to each other. Include the following:**

1. How far apart do they stand or sit?

2. If person A moves closer to person B, what does person B do? If person A moves away from person B, what does person B do?

3. Does person B seem comfortable or uncomfortable? Make notes on B's posture, gestures, facial expressions, and eye movement.

4. Indicate how much you think the following factors night affect the behavior of the people you are observing:

   - whether they are both the same sex
   - whether they are both the same age
   - whether they are both from the same country or same ethnic group
   - how well they know each other

THE FIRST DRAFT
Learning about Writing I

DEVELOPING A THESIS

In Unit One you learned that unity is a very important characteristic of a well-written essay. In the following exercises you will learn about another important characteristic of a well-written essay: the thesis. The thesis is what the writer wants to tell the reader; the writer's purpose in writing. It expresses the main idea of the essay and helps the writer create a unified essay. For example, the subject of selection I, "How Late Is Late?" is the concept of lateness. Its thesis, however, is that ideas about punctuality vary from culture to culture, and that this variation can often result in misunderstanding. The thesis is what the author tells you about the subject of the essay.

Exercise 1: Identifying the Thesis

Look again at selection II, "How Space Communicates: Interaction Distance," on page 23.

1. What is the subject of this selection?

2. What is the main idea or thesis?

Exercise 2: Selecting the Thesis

Each pair of paragraphs below is part of a longer essay. The sentences in the paragraphs are all related to a main idea or thesis that is not stated.

A. Read the first pair of paragraphs. Then decide which of the two groups of sentences that follow (1 or 2) tells you the writer's thesis.

Jamaica offers one example of how close people like to be. In Jamaica, we might stand only a few inches apart when we speak to each other. Two women might even sit so that their heads are touching when they talk. If someone stands twenty inches away, that person seems disrespectful to us. We think that person is cold and standoffish.

The United States is different. In the United States, people are not comfortable standing as close as we do in Jamaica. Americans sometimes feel that Jamaicans are breathing down their necks. Our idea of what is the right social distance makes Americans feel funny. They think that something is wrong with us.

The Writer's Thesis

1. We think that a person who stands too far away isn't worth taking the trouble to talk to. We're sure that person isn't interested in us.

2. Interaction distance is the distance between people when they meet and talk. Not everyone is comfortable with the same distance.

B. Read the second pair of paragraphs. Then decide which of the two groups of sentences that follow (1 or 2) tells you the writer's thesis.

An American friend invited me to her house for dinner at 7:00. I arrived five minutes before 7:00, the way I would in Japan. My friend wasn't ready, and she was upset to see me so early. Most of the other guests didn't arrive until 7:15 or even 7:30.

If that happened to me in Japan, I would think my guests were very rude. When it got to be late and no one was there, I might worry that they had forgotten the date or that something terrible had happened to them. I would not expect to see them at the door at 7:30. And I especially would not expect them to look as though that was the normal time to arrive.

The Writer's Thesis

1. People from different backgrounds don't always view time in the same way. What is late for one person might be early for another.

2. The American guests who arrived at 8:00 seemed terribly rude to me. Didn't they know how insulting it was to be late?

A general statement that contains the main idea, or states the thesis, of an essay is called a *thesis statement*. The thesis statement clarifies the purpose of the essay. It controls the particular set of details that will be included and often indicates how the essay is going to be organized. Developing a thesis is important for guiding you as you write.

Exercise 3: Using the Thesis Statement to Control the Content of an Essay

Each thesis statement below is followed by three descriptions of essays. Select the description that best matches the content and organization suggested by the thesis statement.

1. Thesis Statement: You can be a newcomer, surprised by and unprepared for what you find, without leaving your native land.
   a. an essay that compares the experiences of a woman from Turkey who travels to Holland with the experiences of a woman from the United States who travels to China
   b. an essay that tells how the author adjusted to new experiences such as leaving home for the first time, moving from a farm to a large city, and going to work in a factory
   c. an essay that explains how to prepare for travel to faraway places that are exotic or dangerous

2. Thesis Statement: Two people can misunderstand each other's behavior if they are from two cultures that have different definitions of lateness.
   a. an essay that tells why the author's way of handling punctuality is superior to those of the people with whom the author works
   b. an essay that describes what happened the day the author missed the train and was very late for a business appointment
   c. an essay that compares the way two people handle punctuality and explains how each one feels about the other's behavior

One kind of thesis statement draws a conclusion about the information in the essay, the way the thesis statement you selected in Part B of Exercise 2 does (see page 28). It makes a general statement that is supported by the details in the paragraphs.

Exercise 4: Developing and Stating a Thesis That Draws a Conclusion

For each group of notes below, develop a thesis that draws a conclusion about the information given. Make your thesis into a statement.

Group A

- American women treat both men and women the same way when it comes to interaction distance.
- An American woman will stand a foot or more away from the person she is talking to.
- She is comfortable at this distance and talks in a normal tone of voice.
- The distance is the same, whether she is talking to a man or a woman.
- Jamaican women behave differently.
- Jamaican women don't stand as close to men as they do to women.
- Two Jamaican women will stand as close as five or six inches to each other.
- They don't feel uncomfortable at this distance.
- If she is talking to a man, a Jamaican woman stands about two feet away.
- She feels uncomfortable if she is any closer.
- She will move away or turn her head away.

Thesis Statement: _____

_____

Group B

- In Japan someone who is just a minute late for a business meeting is definitely not on time.
- He or she has to make a slight apology.
- If a Japanese person is seven minutes late, a full apology is needed.
- That person will be considered insulting if he or she is ten minutes late.
- If you are serious about doing business in Japan, you are never this late.
- In my country, Indonesia, one minute late is not thought of as late.
- At ten minutes, an Indonesian will make a slight apology.
- He or she might blame the traffic.
- An Indonesian can be up to thirty minutes late for a business meeting.
- At this point, a full apology might be made.

Thesis Statement: _____

_____

Another kind of thesis statement includes a definition of a concept or a term that is central to the essay, the way the thesis statement you selected in Part A of Exercise 2 does (see page 28). One reason to include a definition in your thesis statement is that when you write about concepts such as lateness or interaction distance, you need to let your reader know what you mean by these terms. Since these are not easy terms to define, you usually need a few sentences for your definition.

Exercise 5: Writing Definitions

A. Practice writing definitions by defining *late* and *interaction distance*.

Use the lists you made in the two writing warm-ups. If you want to, you can break into small groups and use the inquiry method you tried in Unit One, page 1, to arrive at your definition. You may use one of the following openers to begin your definition:

- Late means arriving . . *after the agreed* ~~or appointed~~ *time*
- Interaction distance is a term used by anthropologists to describe . . *the distance between two people while they're interacting.*

B. Practice writing definitions by defining the term given in capital letters in each paragraph below. Use the information in the paragraph to help you arrive at your definition.

1. A STRANGER might feel uncomfortable about joining an established group. He or she might stand a little outside the group and avoid saying much. A stranger is careful not to touch the other members of the group or to seem overly friendly. He or she always seems a little reserved or guarded, waiting to see what other people will do and say first.

Definition: *newcomer, unfamiliar*

2. In my culture, people hardly ever arrive anywhere at an exact time. I think I am ON TIME for a meeting if I am not more than ten minutes late. Arriving early is rude; it is just as bad as being an hour late. In other cultures, though, I have observed that if a meeting is at 10:00 you must be there one minute before 10:00 to be on time.

Definition: *Different cultures being on time differently*

Exercise 6: Developing Your Thesis

A. By now you probably know which topic—lateness or interaction distance—you want to write about. If not, decide on your topic now. Then look at your prewriting lists and notes and answer each of the questions below.

1. What is your purpose in writing? In general, what would you like to tell your readers about the topic you have chosen?

2. How do you want to begin your essay, with a statement that draws a conclusion about the details or with a definition?

B. Use your answers to the questions above to write one or two sentences that state the thesis of the essay you are going to write. Save this statement. You can use it to start organizing your essay. As you write and revise the essay, you may want to revise your thesis statement, too.

Exercise 7: Organizing Your Essay

A. Compare the two organizational plans below. Discuss how each one organizes the writer's observations. How do they make the similarities and differences clear to the reader?

Organizational Plan 1

Introduction (including statement of your thesis):

Describe person A's actions as examples of your thesis:

Point out that person B is similar to and/or different from person A. Describe person B's actions as examples of your thesis:

Organizational Plan 2

Introduction (including statement of your thesis):

Describe the similarities between person A and person B. Alternate an action of person A's with an action of person B's.

Describe the differences between person A and person B. Alternate an action of person A's with an action of person B's.

B. Choose one of the organizational plans shown above. Make a rough diagram that includes the thesis statement you developed in Exercise 6 and that shows how your observations will fit into the plan you have chosen.

Each section of the diagram can be one or more paragraphs. The purpose of this plan is to make sure that you write an essay that compares and contrasts, not one that just tells a story or describes.

Writing the First Draft

CONTENT

Write the first draft of an essay in which you do one of the following:

- Compare and contrast two people's ideas of what constitutes lateness.
- Compare and contrast two people's ideas of what constitutes appropriate interaction distance.

Remember that the purpose of a first draft is to get your ideas down on paper. A first draft is never perfect or complete.

AUDIENCE

Your audience is a colleague who is interested in this topic but doesn't know much about it. You need to make Edward Hall's ideas clear to your audience. You also need to make it clear that you understand the concept of lateness or of interaction distance.

PROCEDURE

- Choose your topic.
- Think about what you have read, discussed, and observed. Select two people that you have discussed or observed whose actions demonstrate different attitudes toward time or space.
- Use one or more of the prewriting techniques you practiced in Unit One to develop your ideas.
- Decide on your thesis. Then write a thesis statement that either includes a definition of a term or draws a conclusion about what you are going to describe. State your thesis in one or two sentences.
- Use the thesis statement to introduce your essay.
- Be as specific as you can about people's words, actions, gestures, and so on, as you compare and contrast the two people you have chosen.
- Make sure the details you include support your controlling idea, or thesis.
- Write your essay. It should be one or two double-spaced, typed pages or two to three double-spaced, handwritten pages.

THE SECOND DRAFT

Once you have put your ideas on paper, you can read what you wrote and begin the process of revision. When you revise, you add to, delete from, change, or reword the first draft.

Learning about Writing II

TOPIC SENTENCES

In addition to having a thesis that holds all the ideas together, an essay usually has a main idea for each paragraph, or subgroup of ideas. The general statement that contains the main idea of the paragraph is called a *topic sentence*.

Exercise 1: Identifying Topic Sentences

For each paragraph below, choose the most appropriate topic sentence.

A. If I had an appointment for a job interview at 2:00 in the afternoon, I would probably be there a few minutes ahead of time. I wouldn't want to offend the person I was meeting by being late. However, if someone invited me to a party at 8:00 P.M., I would know that the invitation really meant some time after 8:00. If I got there around 8:15 or 8:20, it would be fine.

1. I have a lot of appointments that I need to be on time for.

2. The word *late* has no meaning, so it is impossible to be late for anything.

3. An acceptable arrival time in one situation may be considered late in another situation.

B. When I was in high school in Taiwan, I used to go shopping with my girlfriends after school. We always walked arm-in-arm or held hands. In the United States, though, I never see teenage girls walking like this, even if they are sisters. They seem to feel uncomfortable about holding hands or being arm-in-arm in public.

1. It is all right for girls to walk arm-in-arm, but it is not all right for boys.

2. Different cultures have different ideas of how close two women should be.

3. I've always liked to spend my free time with my best girlfriends.

A topic sentence does for the paragraph what a thesis statement does for the essay. It indicates why particular details have been included in that paragraph and helps unify the paragraph. The topic sentence is often the first sentence in the paragraph.

Exercise 2: How Topic Sentences Fit in an Essay

Look at the chart on the next page. It shows one way to organize an essay. Compare the first draft of your essay to the following organizational plan.

- Is your first draft organized in the same way? (Note that the plan below is for a three-paragraph essay; your essay might be a different length.)
- Does your essay contain a sentence that states the main idea of each paragraph?
- Is it related to your thesis? If not, circle anything in your first draft that needs changing, and make a note in the margin about what you plan to do.

Thesis Statement:
one or two sentences that express the controlling idea of the entire essay.
Often part of an introductory paragraph.

Supporting Paragraph 1:
develops an idea that is part of or supports the thesis

    Topic sentence 1: main idea of paragraph 1
    Rest of paragraph 1: details that support topic sentence 1

Supporting Paragraph 2:
develops another idea that is part of or supports the thesis

    Topic sentence 2: main idea of paragraph 2
    Rest of paragraph 2: details that support topic sentence 2

Supporting Paragraph 3:
develops a third idea that is part of or supports the thesis

    Topic sentence 3: main idea of paragraph 3
    Rest of paragraph 3: details that support topic sentence 3

Exercise 3: Stating a Thesis and Writing Topic Sentences

1. Here are prewriting notes that contain details for an essay on time. They
have been grouped to make two paragraphs of the essay.

**Write a topic sentence that states a main idea for each
paragraph. Then write a sentence that states a possible thesis
or controlling idea for the whole essay.**

Veronica

- annoyed if you are one minute late
- walks quickly
- uses instant rice
- makes microwave dinners
- always does two things at once

Annie

- likes to look out window and daydream
- makes her own soup

- never uses a cake mix
- stops to chat with people
- fifteen minutes late is on time for her

Topic Sentence: _____

Topic Sentence: _____

Statement of Thesis: _____

2. Compare the thesis statement and topic sentences you wrote with those of your classmates. Notice that you can develop more than one thesis on the basis of these details. How many ways were there of stating the thesis? How many ways were there of stating the main idea of each paragraph?

Writing the Second Draft

Now that you have waited a few days and had a chance to think about what you have written, you are ready to write the second draft of your essay. Read the first draft again. To help you decide what changes to make, ask yourself the following questions or work with a partner to answer these questions about each other's draft.

- Is there a clear thesis or controlling idea?
- Is the main idea of each paragraph clear?
- Does each paragraph contain details that are related to the main idea?
- Do the details make the actions and feelings of the people you have described clear to your reader? Do you need to add any details?
- Are there any details that don't belong? Is your essay unified?
- Does this essay compare and contrast?

Make whatever changes you need in order to make your thesis clear, unify your essay, and strengthen your comparisons and contrasts. You may need to add, take out, or move some details. As you revise your draft, make sure that you keep your thesis in mind.

Writing the Final Copy

When you are finished revising, edit your essay for errors in spelling, grammar, and punctuation. If you have not already given your essay a title, add one now. Copy your revised draft neatly on clean paper before you hand it in to your instructor.

UNIT THREE
SUMMARIZING AND REACTING TO WHAT YOU HAVE READ

Philosophy

In this unit you are going to read selections from the works of four philosophers. The first three selections answer the question, "What is a good or moral person?" The last selection answers the question, "What makes people act morally?" As you read and discuss these selections, think about your own concept of goodness and of right and wrong.

In Unit Two, observing the actions of other people gave you ideas for your writing. In this unit, you will get ideas for your writing by reading and reacting to what other people have written. Your writing assignment will be to summarize and react to one philosopher's definition of goodness.

GETTING READY TO WRITE

I. What Is a Good or Moral Person?

Meng-tzu (371–289 B.C.), one of the most famous followers of Confucius, was born a little over 100 years after the death of Confucius. He tried to persuade the princes and kings he advised to put into practice the Confucian ideal of ruling through goodness. In this selection you will learn the four virtues Meng-tzu considered the most important.

Before you read the selection from the *Book of Meng-tzu*, think about these questions and discuss your answers with your classmates.

1. What is a good person? How does a "good" person act? What does this person do? On the lines below, list the words, phrases, and images that come to mind.

A Good Person

_____   _____

_____   _____

_____   _____

_____   _____

Compare your list with those of others in your class. What kinds of things do you have in common? What things are different? Are the differences personal ones or are they based on culture? How can you tell? After the discussion you may want to revise your list.

2. Use your revised list to complete the following definitions.

   A good person is someone who . . .

   The culture I was brought up in defines a good person as someone who . . .

3. Are people born with a sense of what is good? If not, how do they acquire it?

4. What is the most important human virtue?

5. Does knowing what is "good" make it easy to do the right thing?

THE FOUR BASIC VIRTUES

All human beings have a capacity for compassion. The real kings of old were compassionate human beings, and so theirs was a government by compassionate men. And having thus brought order to the world, they turned it on the palm of their hands. It can be said that all men have a capacity for compassion because even today if one chances to see a toddler about to fall into a well, one becomes apprehensive and sympathetic. This is not because one knows the child's parents; it is not out of desire for the praise of neighbors and friends; and it is not out of dislike for the bad reputation that would ensue if one did not go to the rescue.

In the light of all this we can conclude that without compassion one would not be a human being. And the same holds if there is no sense of shame, no ability to yield to others, no sense of what is correct and what is not correct. The sense of compassion marks the beginning of becoming man-at-his-best. The sense of shame marks the beginning of propriety. Submissiveness marks the beginning of a sense of ceremony. The sense of right and wrong is the beginning of wisdom. Every human being possesses these four beginnings just as he possesses four limbs. Anyone possessing these four and claiming that he cannot do what they require is selling himself short. If he claims that his prince cannot do what they require, he is selling his prince short. Since, in general, the four beginnings exist within us, it remains only to learn how to enlarge them and bring them to a fullness. This may be compared to the first flicker of a fire, or the first trickle of a spring. If these beginnings can be brought to fullness, one can become protector of the whole world. If they are not brought to fullness, one will be incapable of serving his parents as he should.

THINK AND DISCUSS

Think about the following questions and discuss them with your classmates.

1. What proof does Meng-tzu give that all human beings are compassionate? Read aloud the lines that tell you so.

2. What are the other three virtues according to Meng-tzu? Does everyone possess them?

3. Give an example from modern life to illustrate each of the four virtues.

4. What does Meng-tzu think about people who cannot practice these four things?

The Greek philosopher Aristotle (384–322 B.C.) followed the tradition of using logic or reason to explore all aspects of human knowledge and behavior. He taught by asking questions and encouraging his students to ask questions in return. The end point of this method was to arrive at exact and well-constructed definitions, which he believed to be a reflection of an absolute, universal truth.

Before you read the selection from Aristotle's *Nicomachean Ethics*, discuss the following questions with your classmates.

1. What is self-love? Is it a good quality to have?

2. Who benefits when you do things to improve yourself?

3. Does your culture honor a person who sacrifices his or her own life for the sake of others?

4. What makes most people do the right thing?

SELF-LOVE

The question is debated whether a man should love himself most, or someone else. People criticize those who love themselves most, and call them self-lovers, using this as a term of disgrace. Furthermore, a bad man seems to do everything for his own sake, and the more he does so the more wicked he is and the more others reproach him for it. The good man, on the other hand, acts for honor's sake and acts for his friend's sake, often sacrificing his own interests, and the more he does so the better he is.

Those who use the term "self-love" as a term of reproach ascribe self-love to people who give themselves the greater share of wealth, honors, or of bodily pleasures, since these are what most people desire and busy themselves about. Most men are of this nature, which is why self-love has become a bad term and men who are lovers of self in this way are reproached for being so. But if a man is always anxious that he himself, above all things, should act justly, temperately, or in accordance with the virtues, and in general always tries to follow an honorable course, no one calls that man a lover of self or blames him. But such a man would seem more than the other a lover of self; at all events he assigns himself the things that are noblest and best. And if all were to strive towards what is noble and strain every nerve to do the noblest deeds, everyone would benefit.

Therefore the good man should be a lover of self (for he himself will profit by doing noble deeds and will also benefit others). But the wicked man should not be a lover of self, for he will hurt both himself and his neighbor because he follows his own evil passions. What the wicked man does clashes with what he ought to do. What the good man ought to do he does, for the good man obeys his reason. The good man also does many good acts for the sake of his friends and his country. If necessary, he dies for them. He will throw away wealth, honors, and life itself to gain nobility. He prefers a short period of intense pleasure to a long one of mild enjoyment—a twelve-month of noble life to many years of humdrum existence—and one great and noble action to many trivial ones.

THINK AND DISCUSS

Think about the following questions. Then discuss them with your classmates.

1. According to Aristotle, why does the term *self-love* usually have a negative meaning?

2. What positive meaning does Aristotle give to the term *self-love*? Read aloud the lines that tell you so.

3. Give an example from modern life to illustrate both the good and the bad kind of self-love.

4. According to Aristotle, both the good man and the wicked man know how they should behave. Explain in your own words how Aristotle describes the difference between the two.

5. What are the most important goals in the life of a good man?

The final reading is taken from the sayings of Jesus Christ (A.D. 1–33), whose teachings form the basis of the Christian religion. Jesus was a traveling preacher and healer who reached out to the common person by speaking in simple language and by telling stories to get his point across. After his death, his followers gathered the stories and sayings into a collection of writings known as the *New Testament*.

**Before you read the selection from the *New Testament*,
discuss the following questions with your classmates.**

1. What does the term *revenge* mean to you? How should a good person treat his or her enemies?

2. Is someone who does not stand up for his or her rights a weak person or a strong one? Why?

3. Are good deeds ever rewarded? If so, how?

4. What does it mean to be merciful?

 # THE GOLDEN RULE

Love your enemies, do good to those who hate you.

Bless those who curse you, pray for those who tell lies about you.

And if someone strikes you on one cheek, offer the other also; and if someone takes away your cloak, give him your coat as well.

Give to everyone who asks of thee, and do not ask for a return.

And even as you wish people to do to you, so also you do to them.

For if you love those who love you, what merit have you? For even the wicked love those who love them.

And if you do good to those who do good to you, what merit have you? For even sinners do that.

And if you lend to those from whom you hope to receive in return, what merit have you? For even the wicked lend to the wicked and they may get back as much in return.

But love your enemies; and do good, and lend, not hoping for any return, and your reward will be great, and you shall be called children of the Highest, for He is kind to the ungrateful and to the evil.

Be merciful, therefore, even as your Father is merciful.

Do not judge, and you shall not be judged. Do not condemn, and you shall not be condemned. Forgive and you shall be forgiven.

Give, and it shall be given to you in good measure.

THINK AND DISCUSS

Think about the following questions. Then discuss them with your classmates.

1. This section of Christ's teachings is filled with paradox—statements that seem to contradict each other. "Love your enemies" is one example. Read aloud and discuss four others. Which ones make sense to you? Which ones do not? Why?

2. What reason or reasons does Jesus give for recommending such paradoxical behavior?

3. What reward does he promise to those who follow his suggestions?

4. Are these ways of behaving practical in today's world? Why or why not? Give examples from your own observation or reading to support your answer.

5. Would someone who followed these suggestions consider it wrong to fight?

6. If you suddenly became a leader of your country, which of the behaviors suggested by Meng-tzu, Aristotle, or Jesus would you as a leader practice? Why? Which would you want the leaders of other countries to practice? Why? Which would you want the people of your country to practice? Why?

WRITING WARM-UP

In two or three sentences, write the main idea of one of the three selections you have read.

_____

_____

_____

_____

II. What Makes People Act Morally?

The English philosopher John Stuart Mill taught the doctrine of Utilitarianism. This doctrine was based on the idea that we can determine what is right or moral by determining what brings the greatest happiness to the most people. By "happiness" Mill meant joy, peace, and satisfaction and not the "lower pleasures" of food, drink, or frivolous pastimes.

Mill said that people are persuaded to do the right thing by means of sanctions; that is, by rewards or punishments. Sanctions can be external, such as a fear of being punished or the hope of approval from others. They can also be internal, such as a feeling of discomfort or a feeling of satisfaction.

Before you read the selection from _Sanctions and the Utilitarian Philosophy_, discuss these questions with your classmates.

1. What makes you act morally? For example, what keeps you from taking something that doesn't belong to you or from doing something cruel to a friend?

2. How do you feel when you have acted wrongly? Would you feel differently if you were sure no one would ever know what you did?

3. Do you believe that only the fear of punishment keeps most people from doing wrong or evil things?

THE CONSCIENTIOUS FEELINGS OF MANKIND

The question is often asked, and properly so, in regard to any supposed moral standard—What is its sanction? what are the motives to obey it? or more specifically, what is the source of its obligation? whence does it derive its binding force? It is a necessary part of moral philosophy to provide the answer to this question; which, though frequently assuming the shape of an objection to the utilitarian morality, as if it had some special applicability to that above others, really arises in regard to all standards. . . .

The principle of utility either has, or there is no reason why it might not have, all the sanctions that belong to any other system of morals. Those sanctions are either internal or external. Of the external sanctions it is not necessary to speak at any length. They are the hope of favor and the fear of displeasure from our fellow creatures or from the Ruler of the Universe. . . .

. . . The internal sanction of duty, whatever our standard of duty may be, is one and the same—a feeling in our mind; a pain, more or less intense, attendant on violation of duty, which in properly cultivated moral natures rises, in the more serious cases, into shrinking from it as an impossibility. This feeling . . . is the essence of Conscience . . .

The ultimate sanction, therefore, of all morality (apart from the external motives) being a subjective feeling in our own minds, I see nothing embarrassing to those whose standard is utility, in the question, what is the sanction of that particular standard? We may answer, the same as that of all the other moral standards—the conscientious feelings of mankind. Undoubtedly this sanction has no binding efficacy on those who do not possess the feelings it appeals to. But neither will these persons be more obedient to any other moral principle than to the utilitarian one. On them morality of any kind has no hold but through the external sanctions . . .

THINK AND DISCUSS

Think about the following questions. Then discuss them with your classmates.

1. Mill states that every moral standard should be judged, at least in part, by its sanction. Do you agree with this? Why or why not?

2. Mill mentions two external sanctions. What are they? Give examples of other external sanctions that persuade people to act morally. If you use an idea or an example from one of the other selections in this unit, be sure to say where it came from.

3. What are some examples of internal sanctions that motivate people to act morally? You may use ideas or examples from the other selections.

4. Which is the more moral person according to Mill, the one who acts morally because of external sanctions or the one who follows internal sanctions? Support your answer with an example from the reading.

5. Could there be a situation in which the greatest happiness for one group of people causes unhappiness to another group? If so, what is it?

WRITING WARM-UP

Write a few sentences defining the term "sanctions." Start your definition in one of the following ways:

According to John Stuart Mill, sanctions are . . .

The term "sanctions" refers to . . .

Sanctions can be defined as . . .

_____

_____

_____

_____

PREWRITING

Your assignment for this unit is to discuss and comment on one of the philosophies you have read. The prewriting exercises that follow are designed to help you decide which philosophy to write about. They will also help you clarify your own ideas about the subject of goodness and morality.

Look back at the definitions you wrote at the beginning of this unit and think about the class discussions. Think about your own ideas about moral behavior. Then answer the questions below. Write your answers on the chart on the next page. Choose one of the philosophers and answer the questions as you think he would. Add those answers to the chart.

1. How does a good or moral person live, act, and think?

2. How does a bad or immoral person differ from a good one?

3. What makes a good person act morally?

4. Sanctions are the *shoulds* and *should nots* of a culture. What kind of sanctions do you associate with the following?

   a. wealth

   b. value of human life

   c. the poor

   d. power and the ability to control others

   e. physical pleasures — eating, drinking, etc.

   f. being a trustworthy person

The Good Person

Your Name _____	Philosopher's Name _____

1. _____   1. _____

_____   _____

_____   _____

2. _____   2. _____

_____   _____

_____   _____

3. _____   3. _____

_____   _____

_____   _____

4a. _____   4a. _____

_____   _____

_____   _____

4b. _____   4b. _____

_____   _____

_____   _____

4c. _____   4c. _____

_____   _____

_____   _____

4d. _____   4d. _____

_____   _____

_____   _____

4e. _____   4e. _____

_____   _____

_____   _____

4f. _____   4f. _____

_____   _____

_____   _____

Compare the answers. In what ways do you agree with the philosopher? In what ways do you disagree? Do you think you can write a paper about his philosophy? Could you discuss the philosopher's ideas of morality and state how and why you agree or disagree with them? If not, choose another philosopher and do the exercise again.

THE FIRST DRAFT
Learning about Writing I

Before you discuss someone's ideas, you must tell your reader what those ideas are. Even when your reader has read the same selections you are going to write about, it is important to state which particular ideas you are discussing. One way is to quote the writer's exact words. Another way is to paraphrase or summarize these ideas.

PARAPHRASING

Paraphrasing restates something using new words. When you paraphrase, you include all the information in the original statement; however, you do not use the author's words. A paraphrase may be a bit longer than an original because a new term may need to be explained.

Exercise 1. Putting Ideas into Your Own Words

Look back at the Think and Discuss questions that follow the reading selection from Meng-tzu. In order to answer questions 2 and 4 you had to paraphrase Meng-tzu's words. In the Think and Discuss section after the selection from Aristotle, you had to paraphrase to answer questions 1 and 2, and the Think and Discuss section after the selection from the *New Testament* required a paraphrase of Jesus' words in answer to questions 2 and 3.

A. Compare each paraphrase with its original and write your answers to these questions:

- What did you change?
- What did you add or subtract from the original?
- Which is longer, the paraphrase or the original?

B. Look at the Prewriting questions on page 44. Ask a partner to answer questions 1, 2, and 3. Take notes. When he or she has finished, think about what you have heard. Then paraphrase your partner's answers in writing. Do not use your partner's exact words. You may use one of the following openers to begin your paraphrase:

- (*Partner's name*) believes that . . .
- According to (*partner's name*) . . .
- A good person, according to (*partner's name*) . . .

If you do not remember what your partner said, ask for the answer again. Then ask your partner to check your paraphrase for accuracy and completeness.

Plagiarism is copying exactly or paraphrasing someone else's writing without citing (or naming) the original writer. In your college work you must be careful to cite anyone whose ideas you use. Otherwise you may be accused of plagiarism. There are many different ways to cite the originator of an idea. When you paraphrase you can use the following kinds of phrases to indicate the source of your idea:

- *According to* Aristotle
- Meng-tzu *believed that*
- Jesus *encouraged his followers to*
- Mill *said that*

Exercise 2. Paraphrasing a Text

Look at examples A and B below. Example A is taken from the selection by John Stuart Mill. Example B is a paraphrase. Compare the two. Then answer the questions that follow.

A. The internal sanction of duty, whatever our standard of duty may be, is one and the same—a feeling in our own mind; a pain, more or less intense, attendant on violation of duty, which in properly cultivated moral natures rises, in the more serious cases, into shrinking from it as an impossibility.

B. Mill says that the internal sanction of morality, no matter what moral code we follow, is the same—it is a mental feeling, a more or less severe pain which occurs when we act wrongly. This pain makes very moral individuals so uncomfortable when they think of committing a really serious wrong that it seems impossible to do so.

1. Which is longer, the original or the paraphrase?

2. How does the writer of the paraphrase cite the original author?

3. What words in the original were not changed in the paraphrase? Why do you think the writer did not change them?

4. How were the following phrases paraphrased in example B?

   a. "the internal sanction of duty"

_____

   b. "whatever our standard of duty"

_____

   c. "a feeling in our own mind"

_____

d. "attendant on violation of duty"

e. "properly cultivated moral natures"

f. "in the more serious cases"

Exercise 3. Writing a Paraphrase for Your Paper

Paraphrase part of the text of the philosopher you have decided to write about. Read your paraphrase aloud. Can your classmates identify the source? If they can't, compare your paraphrase to the text and try writing it again.

SUMMARIZING

The texts you paraphrased above were short, and the paraphrases were about the same length. When you summarize, you condense a longer piece of writing into something much shorter. You include the author's purpose and the most important ideas, but you leave out most of the supporting details unless they are necessary for clarifying the author's purpose.

Exercise 4. Practicing Summarizing

Reread the selection from John Stuart Mill on page 43. Then write one or two sentences in answer to the questions below. Your answers should be complete sentences. In the next exercise you will combine the answers to make a paragraph.

1. Which of the following best describes Mill's purpose in writing this selection?
   a. To define the word *sanction* and discuss what the sanctions — or rewards and punishments — of a moral code are
   b. To discuss the difference between internal sanctions and external sanctions
   c. To point out that people obey the utilitarian code for the same reasons they obey any other kind of moral code

2. What is the most important idea in the first paragraph?

3. What is Mill's purpose in the second paragraph?

4. Mill divides the topic of the second paragraph into two parts. What are they?

5. What does Mill say about external sanctions?

6. What is the most important idea in the third paragraph?

7. What is the most important idea in the fourth paragraph? How is it related to Mill's purpose in writing the selection?

Exercise 5. Writing a Summary

Read over your answers from Exercise 4. Use your answers to write a summary paragraph of the John Stuart Mill selection. You will probably have to change some words or add words such as *and, but, because, if* to make the paragraph read smoothly. Remember to put things in your own words by paraphrasing. When you are through, you will have nine or ten sentences which summarize the reading selection.

Writing the First Draft

CONTENT

Write the first draft of an essay that answers the following question:

Which of the philosophies presented in this unit comes closest to your own sense of morality and your own ideas about what makes people follow a moral code?

Summarize the writing of one philosopher and comment on it by comparing his philosophy to your own. Remember that the purpose of a first draft is to get your ideas down on paper. A first draft is never perfect or complete.

AUDIENCE

Your first audience is yourself. Putting your own ideas in writing will help clarify what you think about morality and ethical behavior. The second audience is your fellow students. Even though they have read the same philosophers as you, they do not know what you think is important or how you interpret an idea. Your summaries and paraphrases should be complete and accurate and should emphasize those ideas that you feel come closest to your own.

PROCEDURE

- Decide which philosopher's ideas come closest to your own beliefs.
- Summarize the philosopher's points and use the summary as the introduction to your essay. Begin the introduction with a general statement that characterizes the philosopher's viewpoint and briefly state your opinion of it. This statement will serve as your thesis statement.
- Support your thesis with specific examples drawn from class discussion or incidents you have experienced or observed. Use the chart you completed on page 45 as a source of ideas.
- You may wish to conclude with a short paragraph in which you comment on what makes people behave morally.
- Write your essay. It should be one to two double-spaced, typed pages or two to three double-spaced, handwritten pages.

THE SECOND DRAFT

Remember that the purpose of a first draft is to get your ideas down on paper. In order to complete your essay you have to write a second draft by adding, taking out, or changing material.

Learning about Writing II

SUPPORTING THE THESIS

A good thesis statement tells your reader the conclusions you have come to about a particular subject. A thesis statement alone, however, is usually not enough to convince your reader that your conclusions are accurate or that they make sense. You must choose specific and concrete examples to help make your point clear and to help your reader understand.

In Units One and Two you learned to support your thesis by using examples from your own observation and experience. Now you are going to use someone else's ideas as well as specific examples from your own experience. The next few exercises will give you practice in choosing and using concrete examples.

Exercise 1. Supporting General Statements with Concrete Examples

In writing about philosophy, you often need to make very general statements about good and evil, right and wrong, and so forth. There is nothing wrong with using general statements; however, you need to support or explain them by providing specific examples so that your reader knows exactly what you mean.

The general statements below are all taken from the reading selections. Read them. Then write an example to support or explain each statement. Use examples from your own experience or from your reading.

a. "All human beings have a capacity for compassion."

b. "Love your enemies."

c. "The good man acts for the sake of honor."

d. "What the wicked man does clashes with what he ought to do."

e. "Act toward others the way you want them to act toward you."

f. "Sanctions are either internal or external."

g. "Forgive and you shall be forgiven."

h. "The sense of right and wrong marks the beginning of wisdom."

Exercise 2. *Improving an Essay with Specific Examples*

Below is a student essay about Aristotle's idea of virtue. The student has written a clear and well-organized essay but it would be better if she used a few more examples.

Read the essay. Then answer the questions below.

The Habit of Virtue

Aristotle believed that there are two kinds of virtue: intellectual virtue and moral virtue. He said that intellectual virtue is the result of education, while moral virtue is the result of habit. He did not feel that people were born to be good, but only born with the possibility of becoming good. He went on to say that goodness is a choice to act or behave with moderation in all things. He believed that by practicing moral virtue—forming good moral habits—people became virtuous.

From what he said, I don't think Aristotle thought people were born good or bad but rather that they learned to be moral or virtuous. He seemed to feel that the virtuous person makes a choice to do the right thing and practices acting in a moral way until doing the right thing becomes a habit.

I agree with Aristotle about having to choose to be virtuous and then practicing it. In my country there are people who always watch their children and tell them what to do. They don't ever let their children know about anything bad, and the children never have a chance to be tempted. The parents think those children will grow up to be virtuous, but how can they? They don't ever have a chance to practice being good. They are only good because their parents control them. I don't think that is what Aristotle meant about virtue being a habit. You can only form a habit by having a chance or a choice to practice it. For example, you can't form the habit of not stealing if you don't ever have a chance to steal. You have to be tempted and then choose not to steal. That is what virtue is.

1. What is the thesis of this essay? Is it expressed in a single sentence or does the writer express the thesis in several sentences?

2. In which paragraph does the writer summarize what Aristotle said about virtue?

3. In which paragraph does the writer try to explain what Aristotle meant?

4. In which paragraph does the writer react to Aristotle's ideas about virtue? Does she agree or disagree with him? How do you know?

5. Which statements in the third paragraph are general? What example or examples does the writer use to support the general statements? What other examples can you think of?

6. The second paragraph is very general. What example or examples can you think of that show how virtuous behavior becomes a habit?

Exercise 3. Using Specific Examples in Your Own Essay

Work with a partner and discuss the first draft of your essays. Look for places in each other's essays where a specific example would explain a general statement or help the reader understand it better.

A good way to help your partner is to ask what a particular general statement means to the writer. For example, if your partner has written "My father is a kind man," ask the writer, "How is he kind? What kind acts come immediately to your mind?" The final result might be this:

My father is a kind man. He has always set aside some of the family money to help the poor. At every holiday, he makes sure that everyone who works for him has extra money for a special meal . . .

Now rewrite your own essay, adding details or examples wherever they will strengthen your paper.

Writing the Second Draft

You have made some important changes in your essay, but there are probably some things you could do to improve it even more. Read your essay again and use the questions below to help you decide what additional changes to make.

- Is the thesis clearly stated?

- Does each paragraph support or give more information about the thesis? Does each paragraph have a topic sentence?

- Have you summarized the major points in the selection you have chosen?

- Have you paraphrased clearly and cited the writer?

- Do your specific examples really support or explain the general statements? Are there enough specific examples to make your meaning clear to the reader?

Make whatever changes are necessary to make your thesis clear, summarize and paraphrase correctly, and provide examples that explain your position.

Writing the Final Copy

When you are finished revising, edit your essay for errors in spelling, grammar, and punctuation. If you have not already given your essay a title, add one now. Copy your revised draft neatly on clean paper before you hand it in to your instructor.

UNIT FOUR
RESPONDING TO LITERATURE

Poetry

In this unit you are going to read two poems by the nineteenth-century American poet Emily Dickinson. Both poems are examples of *lyric poetry*, or poetry written to show the poet's feelings or the poet's view of the world. In addition, both poems use images, or pictures, to build comparisons. The first poem compares nature to a gentle mother; the second compares a train to a powerful animal. Your writing assignment will be to discuss the comparison in one of the poems. A paper like this is sometimes called a *critical essay*.

GETTING READY TO WRITE

Think about the words *poem* and *poetry*. What do you already know about poetry? What kinds of poems have you read? Then discuss the questions below with your classmates.

1. What does a poem look like? What does it sound like?
   - Does a poem rhyme?
   - Are the lines of a poem short?
   - Do the lines of a poem look and sound like ordinary sentences?

2. What is a poem about?
   - Does it tell about everyday life?
   - Does it tell about an important person or event?
   - Does it express personal feelings?
   - Does it express a philosophy?
   - Does it guide people in making choices and decisions?

3. How does a poem give its message to the reader?
   - Does it tell a story?
   - Does it paint a picture in words?
   - Does it compare two things, perhaps comparing an abstract idea to something concrete?
   - Does it speak directly to the reader, perhaps giving advice?

4. What is the purpose of poetry?
- To teach the reader something?
- To make the reader feel an emotion?
- To tell a story?

I. A Gentle Mother

When English-speakers use the term "nature," they mean more than just the natural world of mountains and lakes, trees and flowers, birds and animals. They think of nature as an invisible force: something that warms the air of spring or blows up huge waves on the ocean or leads the birds and animals to mate and rear their young. English-speakers sometimes speak about natural events as though they were caused by a being that is almost human—a force that many call "Mother Nature."

In the following poem, Emily Dickinson compares nature to a gentle and loving mother and describes the way nature takes care of her children.

**Before you read "Nature, the Gentlest Mother," think about
what your own mother was like when you were a child.
Then discuss the following questions with your classmates.**

1. How did your mother act when you were naughty?

2. How did she calm you when you were overexcited?

3. What kinds of things did she teach you?

4. What special things did she do when it was time for you to go to bed?

5. What other kinds of things do mothers do for their children?

NATURE, THE GENTLEST MOTHER

1	Nature, the gentlest mother,
2	Impatient of no child,
3	The feeblest or the waywardest,—
4	Her admonition mild
5	In forest and the hill
6	By traveller is heard,
7	Restraining rampant squirrel
8	Or too impetuous bird.

Reprinted by permission of the publishers and the Trustees of Amherst College from The Poems of Emily Dickinson, Thomas H. Johnson, ed., Cambridge, Mass.: The Belknap Press of Harvard University Press, Copyright 1951, © 1955, 1979, 1983 by the President and Fellows of Harvard College.

9	How fair her conversation,
10	A summer afternoon, —
11	Her household, her assembly;
12	And when the sun goes down
13	Her voice among the aisles
14	Incites the timid prayer
15	Of the minutest cricket,
16	The most unworthy flower.
17	When all the children sleep
18	She turns as long away
19	As will suffice to light her lamps;
20	Then, bending from the sky,
21	With infinite affection
22	And infiniter care,
23	Her golden finger on her lip,
24	Wills silence everywhere.

READING STRATEGIES

Although this is a short poem, you may have difficulty understanding it the first time you read it. Read the poem again. This time, use the strategies below to help make the poem clearer. Work with a classmate to discuss each group of questions.

1. One reason the poem is difficult is that the author does not always use the usual English word order. Another reason is that she sometimes leaves out words. Look at lines 4, 5, and 6. If the missing words were added and the usual word order used, these lines would read:

> Her mild admonition is heard by the
>
> traveler in the forest and on the hill.

Where else has the poet changed the word order? Where else have words been left out? How would the lines read if the word order were normal and the missing words were added?

2. Each group of four lines in this poem is called a *stanza*. When you read the poem, do not assume that each line of each stanza is a sentence. Instead, read each group of lines that ends in a semicolon (;) or a period (.) as a sentence. Here is an example of a sentence from lines 17 through 19:

> When all the children sleep
>
> She turns as long away
>
> As will suffice to light her lamps;

Find another example of a group of lines that end in a semicolon. Read them aloud and drop your voice at the end, the way you do at the end of a sentence in English.

3. If a line ends in a comma or has no punctuation at the end, keep reading until you come to a semicolon or a period. Sometimes you will have to continue from the end of one stanza to the beginning of the next in order to reach the end of the sentence. Here is an example from lines 12 through 16:

> And when the sun goes down
> Her voice among the aisles
> Incites the timid prayer
> Of the minutest cricket,
> The most unworthy flower.

How many sentences are there in the last two stanzas of the poem? Where does each sentence begin? Where does each one end?

4. It may help you to understand the poem if you rewrite it in the usual English, in what we call *prose*. To do this, you need to add any words that have been left out and change the order of the words into the usual English order. You may want to look up unfamiliar words in the dictionary as well and use a more familiar word in your prose version. Here is an example of a prose version of the last few lines of the poem:

> Then, bending from the sky with great affection and greater care, with her golden finger on her lip, she orders silence everywhere.

Notice that writing a prose version is similar in some ways to writing a paraphrase like the ones you wrote in Unit Three. Write a prose version of any parts of the poem you find difficult to understand.

THINK AND DISCUSS

Think about the following questions. Then discuss them with your classmates.

1. Lyric poems express personal feelings. What feeling does Dickinson express in this poem?

2. This poem is broken into stanzas that each have the same number of lines. The second and fourth lines of some of the stanzas rhyme. For example, in the first stanza, the last word in line 2 is *child*. It rhymes with *mild*, the last word of line 4. What words rhyme in the other stanzas? Which stanzas contain words at the end of the second and fourth lines that have similar sounds but are not exact rhymes?

3. Which of Nature's "children" does the poet name in the poem? On the board, list the "children." Then, next to each "child," list the word the poet uses to describe it.

4. How does Nature treat her weak and naughty children?

5. What does she do when the sun goes down?

6. When all the children are asleep, what does Nature do?

7. When she puts her finger on her lip, what does Nature tell the whole world to do?

8. If you were going to write a lyric poem about your mother, what feelings would you express?

WRITING WARM-UP

In a few sentences, write about your idea of motherhood. You might begin, "A mother is someone who . . . " or "A good mother is . . . " Save what you have written. You will use it later.

_____

_____

_____

_____

II. A Powerful Animal

Here is another poem by Emily Dickinson. In this poem, she describes a train pulled by a steam engine as it rushes through the countryside. In order to describe the train, the poet compares it to an animal.

Here are some questions that will guide you in your reading. Discuss them with your classmates.

1. What does a steam-driven train look like? Think about the ones you have seen in real life or in the movies or on television. Try to picture the train in your mind. Describe the power and speed of a steam train, how it sounds, and what it might look like when it is climbing a far-away hill.

2. What kind of animal would you compare a steam train to? What does a train do that is similar to the actions of the animal?

3. Read the poem "I Like to See It Lap the Miles." What animal does Emily Dickinson compare the train to? Remember that the poem will be easier to understand if you read each group of lines that ends in a semicolon as though it were one sentence.

I LIKE TO SEE IT LAP THE MILES

1	I like to see it lap the miles,
2	And lick the valleys up,
3	And stop to feed itself at tanks;
4	And then, prodigious, step
5	Around a pile of mountains,
6	And, supercilious, peer
7	In shanties by the sides of roads;
8	And then a quarry pare
9	To fit its sides, and crawl between,
10	Complaining all the while
11	In horrid, hooting stanza;
12	Then chase itself down hill
13	And neigh like Boanerges;
14	Then, punctual as a star,
15	Stop—docile and omnipotent—
16	At its own stable door.

READING STRATEGIES

**Use the reading strategies below to help you better
understand the poem. Work with a classmate to discuss each
group of questions.**

1. The poet has not left out words in this poem; instead she has interrupted the sentences with adjectives that describe the train. For example, look at "prodigious" in line 4 and "docile and omnipotent" in line 15. Where else has the poet interrupted sentences by inserting words that describe the train? If you find any of these lines confusing, try rereading the poem without the adjectives that interrupt the sentences.

2. The poet has changed the word order in only one line of this poem. Where has the word order been changed? What would the normal word order be?

Reprinted by permission of the publishers and the Trustees of Amherst College from The Poems of Emily Dickinson, Thomas H. Johnson, ed., Cambridge, Mass.: The Belknap Press of Harvard University Press, Copyright 1951, © 1955, 1979, 1983 by the President and Fellows of Harvard College.

3. This poem is a list of things the poet likes to see a train do, but the words "I like to see it" appear just at the beginning of the poem. If any lines are confusing, try adding "I like to see it" before the verb. Here is an example from line 12:

> [I like to see it] . . . chase itself down hill

4. Working with your partner, write a prose version of any parts of the poem you find hard to understand. When you write the prose version, remember to ignore the commas at the ends of lines and treat the semicolons as periods. Look up any words you do not understand.

THINK AND DISCUSS

Think about the following questions. Then discuss them with your classmates.

1. This poem is really a long comparison. What does the poet compare the train to? (If you haven't yet decided, look at the last four lines. What animal "neighs" and comes home to a "stable"?)

2. In the poem, Emily Dickinson describes the train's actions with words and phrases that we don't usually use for machines. For example, a train cannot really "step" (see line 4) because it doesn't have feet. A horse, however, can step. What are some of the other things the train does in the poem that are more like the actions of a horse than of a machine?

3. What is the "horrid, hooting stanza" of the train? What do we call a horse's "horrid, hooting stanza"?

4. In line 14, the poet says the train is "punctual as a star." Are stars "punctual"? In what way? Are modern trains as punctual as stars?

5. If you were going to write a poem like this one, what machine would you write about? What would you compare it to? (Choose an animal, a plant, or something else in nature.)

WRITING WARM-UP

We sometimes speak of the train as the "iron horse." In a few sentences, state why a train is like a horse. You might begin, "A train is like a horse because . . . " Save what you have written. You will use it later.

_____

_____

_____

_____

_____

PREWRITING

The words and phrases Emily Dickinson uses to describe nature and the train are called *images*. An image is a picture; in a poem, it is a picture created by words. In order to write an essay that discusses the comparison in one of Dickinson's poems, you need to be able to recognize and describe the images Dickinson uses. You also need to be able to explain whether you think her choice of images is effective. Do the prewriting activities below. They will give you practice in identifying and discussing the images in these two poems. In addition, they will help you decide which poem to write about.

Below are some pictures of mothers and children. They are very different from mothers and children you might see in the United States today, but they are similar to the pictures that were popular in the nineteenth century, when Emily Dickinson lived and wrote. In each picture, the mother is doing something similar to what the poem describes Nature doing for her "children."

A. Look at the pictures. Then, in each space, copy the line or lines from "Nature, the Gentlest Mother" that contain a poetic image that matches the visual image. The first one has been done for you. Save this list to use when you write your essay.

1. *Nature, the gentlest mother, / impatient of no child, / the feeblest or the waywardest, — / her admonition mild*

2.

_____

_____

_____

3.

_____

_____

_____

4.

_____

_____

_____

5. _____
   _____
   _____

6. _____
   _____
   _____

B. Below are some images from the second poem. On the lines below each image, first briefly state what the image shows the train doing. Then describe what a horse would be doing in the same circumstances. The first one is done for you. Save your notes to use when you write your essay.

1. "stop to feed itself at tanks"

train: *stop to have the boiler filled with water from tanks*

horse: *drink water from a watering trough*

2. "step around a pile of mountains"

train: _____

horse: _____

3. "complaining . . . in horrid, hooting stanza"

train: _____

horse: _____

4. "chase itself down hill"

train: _____

horse: _____

5. "stop . . . at its own stable door"

train: _____

horse: _____

THE FIRST DRAFT

Learning about Writing I

ORGANIZING A CRITICAL ESSAY

When you write a critical essay, the piece of literature you are analyzing can often help you organize your ideas. In a poem, for example, the poet uses images to express ideas and feelings. When you discuss the poet's images, the easiest way to organize your essay is to follow the poet's plan, that is, to discuss each image in the order in which it occurs in the poem.

Exercise 1: Identifying the Structure of a Critical Essay

Read the following poem and essay. Then answer the questions.

HOPE IS THE THING WITH FEATHERS

Hope is the thing with feathers
That perches in the soul,
And sings the tune without the words,
And never stops at all,

And sweetest in the gale is heard;
And sore must be the storm
That could abash the little bird
That kept so many warm.

I've heard it in the chillest land,
And on the strangest sea;
Yet, never, in extremity,
It asked a crumb of me.

Hope Springs Eternal

In the poem "Hope Is the Thing with Feathers," Emily Dickinson compares hope to a little bird. Comparing hope to a bird is an excellent way of describing hope. Anyone who has ever seen a little bird hopping around in the branches on a cold winter day or singing its little heart out on a gloomy morning will understand what a good symbol a bird is for the kind of hope that keeps us going when everything seems sad and gloomy.

The poet says hope "perches in the soul" and sings "the tune without the words" without ever stopping. She goes on to say that the song sounds sweetest in the gale. A gale is a terrible wind, and what the poet means here is that we never quite give up hoping that everything will be all right. Hope is always with us, down deep in our souls, and we keep on hoping even when things are really bad. In fact, that little bit of hope in our souls seems the very sweetest when the "gale" of our troubles blows.

In the second stanza the poet says it takes a really bad storm to "abash the little bird, /That kept so many warm." In other words, things have to be really bad before we quit hoping. It is hope that keeps us "warm," or keeps us going when we have troubles.

Reprinted by permission of the publishers and the Trustees of Amherst College from The Poems of Emily Dickinson, Thomas H. Johnson, ed., Cambridge, Mass.: The Belknap Press of Harvard University Press, Copyright 1951, © 1955, 1979, 1983 by the President and Fellows of Harvard College.

The last stanza says the poet has heard the song of hope in "the chillest land, /And on the strangest sea." She means that people keep hoping, even in situations where it seems impossible to hope—situations where you might think the bird of hope would fly away. She concludes by saying that hope has never asked a crumb from her. In other words, hope always perches in our souls, and we don't have to take care of it in any way.

1. What is the thesis of this essay? Is it expressed in a single sentence or does the writer express the thesis in several sentences?

2. What is the writer's purpose in the first paragraph?

3. Which part of the poem does the writer discuss in the second paragraph?

4. Which part of the poem does the writer discuss next?

5. Which part of the poem does the writer discuss last?

6. What strategy does the writer use to organize this essay?

Exercise 2: Creating an Essay Organization Plan

One way of planning how to group your ideas when you write a critical essay is to make an essay organization plan. The writer of the essay in the previous exercise might have made a plan for the body of the essay that began like the one below.

Read this section of the plan and then answer the questions.

Image 1: A little bird perching in the soul and singing without stopping, even in a storm

Explanation: Hope might be small, like a bird, but it is always with us—even when things are bad. When our troubles are worst (the gale), hope is the strongest.

1. What kind of notes did the writer make following the words *Image 1*? What kind of notes did the writer make following *Explanation*?

2. Which paragraph of the essay did these notes become?

Here is the second image in the poem. Add notes to explain it and then answer questions 3 and 4.

Image 2: A terrible storm that might frighten the bird away or stop it from singing

Explanation: _____

_____

3. Which paragraph of the essay would these notes become?

4. How many more images do you think the writer made notes on in order to plan the body of the essay?

Exercise 3: Organizing Your Essay

Reread the poem you plan to write about. Then make an essay organization plan.

First, list the poet's images *in the order in which they occur in the poem*. Leave space after each image for your notes. Then go back and make notes about how you will explain each image or group of images. Each image and explanation will probably become one paragraph in your essay.

Exercise 4: Noting Your Response to the Poem

Explaining the images in a poem is only part of a critical essay. You also need to discuss the effectiveness of these images. To do this, you need to make some additional notes about your personal reaction to the poem—what you think of the poet's choice of images.

1. **Here are some personal-reaction notes the writer of the model essay in Exercise 1 (page 64) made. Where are these notes used in the model essay?**

Personal Reaction
Bird is good image for hope—small and delicate, but it cheers us up with its singing.

2. **Reread the poem you have chosen and the notes you made for your essay organization plan. Then make a new heading at the end of the essay organization plan—*Personal Reactions*. In this section, add some notes that give your reaction to the images Dickinson uses.**

Exercise 5: Stating Your Thesis

When you have completed the plan, look at all your notes. What ideas occur most frequently or seem most important in the explanation of the images? Use these ideas to write the thesis statement for your essay.

Your thesis statement should explain the comparison the poet is making. It should also tell your readers whether you think this comparison is effective.

Exercise 6: Writing an Introduction

Expand the statement of your thesis into an introductory paragraph.

Add details to your explanation of the poet's comparison, and tell why you think the comparison is or is not effective. If you need a model, reread the first paragraph of the essay in Exercise 1 (page 64).

Writing the First Draft

CONTENT

Write the first draft of an essay in which you do one of the following:

- Discuss the comparison and the imagery in "Nature, the Gentlest Mother."
- Discuss the comparison and the imagery in "I Like to See It Lap the Miles."

AUDIENCE

Your audience is your instructor and possibly your fellow students. Even though they have read and discussed the poem, you need to state what the poem is about and use concrete examples from the poem so that the audience will understand your interpretation of it. It is particularly important for you to be clear and concrete in order to show your audience how well you understand and can discuss the poem.

PROCEDURE

- Decide which poem you are going to write about.
- Make a general statement about the poem and its imagery. This statement will be your thesis statement. You can expand your thesis statement into an introductory paragraph that explains why you think the poet's choice of imagery is or is not effective.
- Support your thesis with a discussion of specific images from the poem. Be sure to discuss the entire poem. Reread your notes from the writing warm-up and prewriting activity for ideas about the imagery.
- Organize your paper so that you discuss each image in order. Use the essay organization plan you created in Exercise 3 on page 66 to help you.
- Write your essay. It should be one or two double-spaced, typed pages to two to three double-spaced, handwritten pages.

THE SECOND DRAFT

Remember that the purpose of a first draft is to get your ideas down on paper. In order to complete your essay you have to write a second draft by adding, taking out, or changing material. The exercises below can help you revise.

Learning about Writing II

USING QUOTATIONS FOR SUPPORT

In Unit Three you learned to paraphrase and summarize so that your reader will understand the source of your comments. Another way to let your reader know the source of your ideas is to use the exact words of the writer. Using someone else's words is called "quoting."

Look again at the essay "Hope Springs Eternal" on page 64. In the essay, the writer has quoted a number of phrases from the poem, such as "the thing with feathers," "sweetest in the gale," and "abash the little bird, /That kept so many warm." Each phrase is enclosed in quotation marks ("/"). Quotation marks indicate that the writer is using the poet's exact words.

Exercise 1: Quoting Another Writer

Compare the two paragraphs below. Then answer the questions that follow.

A. In the second stanza the poet says that things have to be really bad before we stop hoping. She points out that hope keeps people warm when things are bad.

B. In the second stanza the poet says it takes a really bad storm, a "gale," to "abash the little bird, /That kept so many warm." In other words, things have to be really bad before we quit hoping. It is hope that keeps us "warm," or keeps us going when we have troubles.

1. Which paragraph gives you a more complete idea of what the poet is saying? What has the writer of this paragraph done to make the poet's imagery more vivid for you?

2. Why did the writer use quotation marks around *gale*, *abash the little bird, /That kept so many warm*, and *warm* in the last line of the paragraph?

3. Compare the quoted words in paragraph B to the second stanza of "Hope Is the Thing with Feathers" on page 64.
    a. What letters are capitalized in the poem? In the paragraph?
    b. What do you think the slash (/) in front of *That* in the paragraph indicates?
    c. Is the period after *warm* in the second line of the paragraph inside or outside the quotation marks?

Exercise 2: Identifying Direct and Indirect Quotations

There are two ways to include someone else's words and ideas in your writing: direct quotations and indirect quotations.

A. Read the two examples below. Then answer the questions to find out how a direct quotation differs from an indirect quotation.

1. Direct Quotation

    Emily Dickinson calls the train's whistle a "horrid, hooting stanza."

The writer has used Dickinson's exact words in this quotation. How has she shown which words are Dickinson's?

2. Indirect Quotation

> Emily Dickinson says that the train's whistle makes a terrible, loud sound.

The writer has used her own words to state Dickinson's idea. Has she used quotation marks? How has she shown that this idea is Dickinson's?

B. Write *D* next to each direct quotation below. Write *I* next to each indirect quotation.

1. Dickinson describes hope as a small feathered creature. _____

2. According to the poet, hope "perches in the soul." _____

3. Emily Dickinson describes hope as a bird that sings "the tune without the words." _____

4. In the last stanza, Dickinson says that she has heard hope singing in the coldest places. _____

5. Dickinson concludes by saying that hope has never asked a thing from her. _____

Remember that when you quote directly, you must use the exact spelling, capitalization, and punctuation of the author. When you quote indirectly, you paraphrase, stating the author's ideas in your own words, without quotation marks. Whether you are quoting directly, with quotation marks, or using an indirect quotation, you must be careful to say whose ideas you are referring to. As you learned in Unit Three, using someone else's ideas without citing your source is plagiarism.

Exercise 3: Writing Direct and Indirect Quotations

Read the paragraph below from *This Was a Poet: A Critical Biography of Emily Dickinson* by George F. Whicher. Following it are five general statements about Emily Dickinson's life. Using the information in the paragraph below, write one or two sentences to support each of the general statements. Write each supporting sentence twice— once as a direct quotation and once as an indirect quotation. The first one is done for you.

The external story of [Emily Dickinson's] life is very nearly a blank. After sharing the normal girlhood experiences of her contemporaries she remained at home, tending her garden. Her farthest travels consisted of several visits to Boston, twice in later years for the care of her eyes, and a short trip to Washington and Philadelphia when she was twenty-three. If at any time she fell upon the thorns of life, she was careful that no one should see her hurt. For the last twenty years that she lived she preferred the seclusion of her father's house to any society that the village or

Excerpt *from* This Was A Poet—A Critical Biography of Emily Dickinson by *George Frisbie Whicher. Copyright* © *1938 by Charles Scribner's Sons. Reprinted by special arrangement.*

the world could offer. To intimate friends she sent vivid letters and occasional bits of verse, but not even the members of her family suspected the work that she was perfecting in secret. Fame she thought a perilous food, and for her own part she would not even nibble of it. Only after her death was her hoard of poems uncovered. Then as increment after increment was published, lovers of poetry gradually came to realize that the most memorable lyric poet in America had lived and died unknown.

1. Emily Dickinson rarely went anywhere.

Direct: Whicher says, "Her farthest travels consisted of several visits to Boston, twice in later years for the care of her eyes, and a short trip to Washington and Philadelphia when she was twenty-three."

Indirect: According to Whicher, she went to Washington and Philadelphia once when she was twenty-three and to Boston a few times. Two of her trips to Boston were made to have her eyes taken care of when she was older.

2. Emily Dickinson was almost a hermit.

Direct: _____

Indirect: _____

3. No one knew about the poems Dickinson was writing.

Direct: _____

Indirect: _____

4. Dickinson was not interested in being famous.

Direct: _____

Indirect: _____

5. Dickinson's work became known only after she had died.

Direct: _____

Indirect: _____

Exercise 4: Using Quotations in Your Own Essay

Working with a partner, exchange your first drafts of the critical essay. Read your partner's essay and tell your partner where the essay can be improved by adding direct quotations from the poem. Then rewrite your own essay. Use your partner's comments to help you add direct quotations wherever they will strengthen your paper.

When you and your partner have both finished revising, exchange papers again. Read each other's revised essays and comment on the following points:

- Is the revised version better and more vivid than the first draft? Do the quotations provide additional support for the points the writer is trying to make?
- Has the writer quoted the original *exactly* (even any oddly spelled words)?
- Is the quoted material punctuated like the original?
- Has the writer indicated the ends of lines correctly?
- Are periods and commas inside the quotation marks?

Writing the Second Draft

You have made some important changes in your essay. But there are probably some things you could do to improve it even more. Read your essay again and use the questions below to help you decide what additional changes to make.

- Is the thesis clearly stated?
- Does the essay follow the plan of the poem?
- Have you supported your thesis with specific examples of the poem's imagery?
- Have you discussed all the images in the poem? Do you need to add any details?
- Are there any details that don't belong? Is your essay unified?
- Is the main idea of each paragraph clearly stated?
- Have you expanded your thesis statement into an introduction?
- Have you explained why the poet's comparison is or is not effective?
- Have you given the author credit for every direct and indirect quotation you have used?

Make whatever changes you need in order to make your thesis clear. Explain the author's images completely, and organize the supporting details logically. You may need to add, take out, or move some details. As you revise your draft, make sure that you keep your thesis in mind.

Writing the Final Copy

When you are finished revising, edit your essay for errors in spelling, grammar, and punctuation. If you have not already given your essay a title, add one now. Copy your revised draft neatly on clean paper before you hand it in to your instructor.

UNIT FIVE
TAKING WRITTEN TESTS

Economics

In this unit, you are going to read two selections from a college economics textbook and take an essay test on what you have read. You will not have to study for this because you can take the test at home, using your book and notes to help you. The purpose of this unit is to help you use what you have learned about writing to answer test questions. Some of the exercises that follow the readings are designed to help you understand what you have read. Others will help you learn some strategies for taking tests.

GETTING READY TO WRITE

I. The Economic Problem

The reading selection below is taken from *Dollars and Sense: An Introduction to Economics*, a college economics textbook written by Marilu Hurt McCarty. Before you read the selection, "Scarcity and Choice," preview the material to identify the most important points. Previewing is an excellent way to examine any selection before you actually read it. Doing so should give you a fairly good idea of the author's thesis, the main topics, and important new terms.

To preview, read the title, the first sentence or paragraph, the headings, and the boldface words. Then discuss the questions below with your classmates and take notes on your answers.

1. What is the selection about? What do you think the author's thesis might be?

2. What are the most important topics in the selection?

3. What are the most important terms the author uses?

Now read the selection carefully.

SCARCITY AND CHOICE

What is an economic system? And why is an economic system necessary?

Throughout the history of life on this planet, human beings have faced the problem of scarce resources: limited supplies of materials, labor, and equipment to produce the goods and services we want. With scarce resources and unlimited wants, we are forced to *choose* the things we want most. We find that to obtain some of the things we want requires us to give up other things we might have had.

If all resources were free—that is, if all of us could have as much as we wanted of everything—we wouldn't need an economic system. There are, in fact, some resources that we might consider free. Fresh air and sunshine are free on a tropical island. Each person can have as much as he or she wants, and there will still be enough for everyone else. In a crowded city, on the other hand, fresh air may be very much a scarce resource. We must pay a price in order to obtain it. The price of pollution control (or of an airline ticket to a tropical island) is an example of the price we might pay. Unfortunately, as we soon discover, most resources are scarce.

Because resources are scarce, they must be used wisely. Every community, whether of cave dwellers or high-rise apartment dwellers, must establish a system for allocating its scarce resources. Resources must be channeled into production of the goods and services the people want most. How much of the scarce land should be used to produce wheat and how much to produce strawberries? How much of the scarce metal resources should be used for autos and how much for airplanes? How much of the scarce labor power should be used to build dams and how much to teach college students?

We can't have all we want of everything. So we must choose the things we want most! That is why we have an economic system. An **economic system** provides a way of choosing.

The Economic Problem

The problem of scarce resources and unlimited wants is called the **economic problem**. We have said that every society faces limits on its ability to satisfy its ever expanding wants. With scarce resources and available technology there are limits to the quantities of goods and services that can be produced. The economic problem requires a society to use its scarce resources efficiently so as to produce the combination of goods and services that most nearly fits the needs and desires of its people.

The Four Kinds of Resources

Productive resources are classified into four groups: land, labor, capital, and management or entrepreneurial ability.

From Dollars and Sense: An Introduction to Economics, 5/e by Marilu Hurt McCarty. Copyright © 1988, 1985 by Scott, Foresman and Company. Reprinted by permission of HarperCollins Publishers.

Land may be thought of as "natural resources." Land includes all the original and nonreproducible gifts of nature: fertile soil, mineral deposits, fossil fuels, and water. All are fixed in amount but, when combined with human ingenuity, may be made to produce wanted goods and services.

In years past the vastness of the earth's natural resources tempted us to regard them as inexhaustible and, therefore, free. Threats of future shortages, however, remind us that we still must avoid wasteful exploitation of our land resources.

Labor may be thought of as "human resources." Labor is the purposeful activity of human beings: teachers, psychiatrists, lathe operators, roustabouts, statisticians. Failure to use productively a single willing hour of labor results in a permanent sacrifice of the good or service that resource might have produced.

Capital may be thought of as "manufactured resources." Capital includes the tools and equipment that strengthen, extend, or replace human hands in the production of goods and services: hammers, sewing machines, turbines, bookkeeping machines, components of finished goods, specialized skills. Capital resources permit "roundabout" production: through capital, goods are produced indirectly by a kind of tool rather than directly by physical labor.

To construct a capital resource requires that we postpone production of consumer goods today so that we may produce more in the future. (Economists do not think of money as capital, since money by itself cannot produce anything at all. However, money is a convenient means of "storing" resources for use in future production.) . . .

Management or **entrepreneurial ability** may be thought of as the "creative resource." Entrepreneurship provides the human initiative that combines other resources to work hard toward a certain goal. Entrepreneurial ability is provided by the owner or developer, creator, or administrator of a productive enterprise.

The entrepreneur plays another role in our economic system. Because the future is not known, the developer or creator of an enterprise must take risks. Entrepreneurs will undertake risks of loss only if they believe there is also the chance of reward. It takes a certain kind of person to agree to be a risk-taker, and the entrepreneur is that type of person.

The first three resources are certainly necessary. But the fourth may be even more critical for producing the largest possible quantity and quality of desired goods and services.

The Three Questions: What? How? For Whom?

A society's stock of resources can be combined in a variety of ways to produce goods and services. To decide how to allocate its resources, a society must answer three basic questions:

The society must first decide **What?** to produce. "How many consumer goods?" might be the choice facing a nation preparing for war. "How many new houses?" and "How many machines?" the critical choice for a developing nation. "How many agricultural products?" and "How many manufactured goods?" the choice for a nation dependent on international trade.

Whatever goods and services the society decides to produce, it must at the same time sacrifice other goods and services it might have chosen.

Second, a society must decide **How?** resources should be combined to produce the desired goods and services. If the society is rich in land, it may decide to emphasize the use of land in production. This was true in our own country in the nineteenth century and is true in Argentina and Australia today. If workers are plentiful, the society may emphasize the use of labor, as in populous Japan. If the society is rich in capital resources, it may emphasize the use of machinery, as in the United States today. A country without fertile land and with few human resources may choose to develop and encourage entrepreneurial ability through training in business management.

Whatever resources the society decides to use in production, it must at the same time sacrifice other goods and services those resources might have produced.

Finally, any society must decide **For Whom?** output is to be produced. Who is to be rewarded at the time goods and services are distributed? Brain surgeons or ballet dancers? Poets or industrial designers? Teachers or soldiers? Often, a worker's reward reflects the value the society places on the good or service that worker produces. A generous reward will encourage greater production of a good or service the society wants most.

Needless to say, whichever workers the society decides to reward generously, it must at the same time reward other workers less well.

THINK AND DISCUSS

Think about the following questions. Then discuss them with your classmates.

1. Reread the notes you took when you previewed this reading selection. How well did you predict what it would be about? If you missed important topics or terms, add them to your notes.

2. Think of something you either need or want very much and answer the questions below:

   a. What resources are required to provide this item?

   b. What is the cost of having this item?

   c. How much demand is there for this item? In other words, how much do other people want it?

   d. How scarce is this item? Can everyone have as much as he or she wants or is the supply limited?

3. Think about something that your city or country provides to people and answer the "three basic questions" about it:

   a. **What** is it? Is it manufactured, such as computers, or is it a natural resource, such as beautiful scenery or wonderful ski hills?

   b. **How** is it provided? What productive resources are required to provide it to people?

   c. **For whom** is it produced?

II. Making Choices

Like "Scarcity and Choice," the reading selection below is from Marilu Hurt McCarty's *Dollars and Sense: An Introduction to Economics*. The application problem that follows it, "What Are the Opportunity Costs of a College Education?" is from another college economics text, *Economics Today* by Roger LeRoy Miller.

Before you read the second selections, work in pairs or small groups to preview the material. Read the title, the first sentence or paragraph, the headings, and the boldface words. Then discuss the following questions and take notes on the answers.

1. What is the reading about? What do you think the author's thesis might be?

2. What are the most important topics in the reading?

3. What are the most important terms the author uses?

CHOICE AND OPPORTUNITY COSTS

Economics is the study of choosing. Regrettably, every choice involves a trade-off: a cost. The cost to use a resource to produce one good or service is the next most desired good or service we might have produced instead. Economists refer to such alternative uses as **opportunity costs**.

The opportunity cost to an athlete of a tennis match is the golf game he or she might have played (or the nap in the shade). The opportunity cost to a homemaker of a loaf of homemade bread is the book he or she might have read (in addition to the alternative uses of the flour, eggs, and other ingredients). The opportunity cost to a college student of intensive study for one course is the "A" he or she might have earned in another.

As consumers, we all make choices based on opportunity costs. With limited financial resources, a decision to spend a dollar for one good means the sacrifice of another good we might have bought instead. The purchase of a new sweater may require the sacrifice of a pair of concert tickets.

Producers consider opportunity costs, too, when employing limited productive resources. When a business firm employs an hour of labor, a piece of machinery, or an acre of land, its managers must consider the alternative uses of these resources. Labor and materials can be used to build schools or bridges, ice rinks or pizza parlors,

From Dollars and Sense: An Introduction to Economics, 5/e by Marilu Hurt McCarty. Copyright © 1988, 1985 by Scott, Foresman and Company. Reprinted by permission of HarperCollins Publishers.

airplanes or trains. The opportunity cost of each is the other good or service not produced. An acre of land used for tennis courts is not available for use as a parking lot!

If the society allocates its resources to produce the most wanted goods and services with the least sacrifice of other goods and services, we say the society is efficient. When we choose efficiently, we hold opportunity costs to a minimum.

Making Choices

The study of economics develops habits of thought that help us choose better—to weigh the benefits of every choice against the opportunity cost and to make efficient decisions.

The economic way of thinking is important to every one of us in our roles as consumers and as producers. As consumers we weigh the benefits of every spending decision against the cost. We compare the benefits of a new car with a family trip to the beach, a night on the town with a new sport jacket, or a motorcyle with a year's membership in a health club. We want to get the most benefit out of every dollar of our limited budgets. As producers we weigh the benefits of every production decision against the costs of resources for producing it. We know that our resources are scarce. So we produce the goods we want with the resources we have in greatest abundance: boats from plentiful fiberglass, wheat from vast Western plains, and clothing from abundant cotton.

Choosing at the Margin

Many of our economic decisions depend on comparisons at the margin. The margin is the edge or border where we must decide whether to take one more step, whether to purchase one more unit of a particular good or whether to use one more unit of a particular resource.

Most of us use **marginal analysis** unconsciously every day. We use marginal analysis when we allocate our time, continuing one activity until the benefits gained from spending one more minute are less than the benefits from spending that minute doing something else. Marginal analysis helps a student allocate study time or a worker allocate work time among a number of tasks. (Even a fun-seeker allocates pleasure time by comparing the benefits gained from spending one more minute of playing with the benefits of spending that minute resting!)

We also use marginal analysis when we allocate our money. We spend for one item until the benefits gained from spending one more dollar are less than the benefits from spending that dollar on something else. A sports fan attends football games only up to the point where he or she believes a bowling match would be more fun.

Business firms use marginal analysis to decide the level of production. An auto manufacturer produces autos until production of one more auto brings in less revenue than it costs to produce. A barber keeps his shop open until one more hour brings in less revenue than the cost of staying open.

Business firms also use marginal analysis to decide how many resources to use in production. They hire salespeople until hiring one more worker adds less to sales revenue than the worker's wage. They buy land for shopping centers until one more acre of space adds less to revenue than it costs.

In effect, our entire economic system makes decisions at the margin. We increase production until one more unit is worth less than the resources required to produce it. In this way we help ensure that our scarce resources are used efficiently.

Economics is the study of choices in the market system . . . .

Application: What Are the Opportunity Costs of a College Education?

An ad in one local newspaper read as follows: "It will cost you $3.34 a day to go to Sunshine College. That's based on today's prices where you will spend $1,068 to attend this community college for two years, including tuition fees and textbooks. It comes out to $3.34 a day." That sounds like a pretty good deal, doesn't it?

A typical college student might look at the cost of going to school as including a little bit more, because the student would pay for food, clothing, and recreation. His or her yearly cost-accounting might be as follows for one year:

1. Tuition and fees:	$ 650	
2. Books:	$ 240	
3. Room:	$1,400	
4. Food:	$1,400	
5. Recreation:	$ 300	
TOTAL:	$3,990 per year[1]	

If you were to multiply this total by four, you would come up with a sizable number, and in this particular example a four-year program would cost 4 × $3,990, or $15,960. . . .

Does $15,960 represent the true cost of going to school for four years? Remember that *the cost of doing anything is its opportunity cost.* Right away you can see that a major cost was left out of the first calculations and, by implication, left out of the very misleading ad for a local community college. The alternative of going to school is working and earning income. If, with the same effort, you could make after taxes, say, $10,000 a year, then the opportunity cost of your time of going to school is $10,000 times the number of years you stay in school. Further, room, board, and recreating do *not* represent a cost of going to school, because you don't have any alternative. You eat, sleep, and have fun no matter what you are doing; thus, the calculation given above is grossly inaccurate. What it should include is (1) the opportunity cost of not working, (2) tuition fees, and (3) textbooks and incidentals related strictly to schooling. The revised figures for one year might look like this:

1. Forgone after-tax earnings:	$10,000 (opportunity cost of your time)	
2. Tuition and fees:	$ 650	
3. Books:	$ 240	
TOTAL:	$10,890 per year	

The full cost of education at this school for four years would then be 4 × $10,890, or $43,560. That's quite a bit more than the original calculation, isn't it? But it's more accurate in terms of the true cost to you as an individual with alternatives in a world of scarcity. . . .

[1] These figures reflect the approximate cost of education at a state university in 1985.

Excerpts from Economics Today, 6/ed. by Roger LeRoy Miller. Copyright © 1988 by Harper & Row, Publishers, Inc. Reprinted by permission of the publisher.

THINK AND DISCUSS

Think about the following questions. Then discuss them with your classmates.

1. Look over your preview notes for these reading selections. How well did you predict what they would be about? If you missed important topics or terms, add them to your notes.

2. In "Choice and Opportunity Costs," the author says that a society that allocates its resources well and gives people the things they want most without making them sacrifice too many other goods is an *efficient* society. Think about your own society. Do you think it is efficient? Why or why not?

3. Think about a decision you need to make this week. Use marginal analysis to make the decision. Do you think you will act on your decision?

4. The opportunity costs of going to college include not only the cost of tuition and books but the cost of the income you don't earn while you are in college. What are the opportunity costs of *not* going to college?

UNDERSTANDING TEST QUESTIONS

No matter what kind of test you take, you cannot write a good answer unless you understand the question and do what the question requires. For example, if the question asks you to *compare* two things but you *discuss* only one of them, you will not get a good grade—no matter how good your discussion is. If the question asks about using marginal analysis to determine production, but you only *define* marginal analysis instead of discussing how it can be used to determine production, you will be marked down for not answering the question.

When you read a test question, you must ask yourself two questions:

1. *What type of question is it?* What does it require you to do? Compare and contrast? Define? Apply what you have learned in order to solve a problem? Summarize? etc.

2. *What content does the question ask about?* The Depression? Unemployment? Inflation? etc.

Types of Test Questions

Below are some of the most common types of test questions. Opposite the name of each type of question is an example and a statement about what the question requires you to do. Because there are many ways to ask the same question, there is also an example of another way to word each question. In the examples, the content—what you are asked to write about—is underlined.

Cause/Effect
Example: What happens in a time of inflation?

Discuss what caused something, what the effects of something are, or what both the causes and the effects are. To answer the question above, you would discuss the effects of inflation.

Another wording: What are the effects of inflation?

Compare/Contrast
Example: Distinguish between a change in demand and a change in quantity demanded.

Discuss how two or more things are similar and how they are different.

Another wording: Compare a change in demand and a change in quantity demanded.

Define
Example: What is the production possibilities frontier?

Tell what something is and what makes it different from other, similar things. Include an example with your definition.

Another wording: Identify the production possibilities frontier.

Evaluate
Example: Evaluate supply-side economics as a solution for inflation.

Discuss what is good and what is bad about something.

Another wording: Is supply-side economics an effective solution for inflation? Why or why not?

Explain
Example: How is GNP (gross national product) computed?

Describe how something works or how to do something. The question above requires you to describe the process of computing GNP.

Another wording: Describe the way GNP is computed.

Summarize
Example: What was Keynes' solution to unemployment?

State the main steps, points, or issues of something—a theory, an historical event, a procedure, etc. Be sure to include all the important points or steps.

Another wording: Explain how Keynes proposed to solve unemployment.

(continued on next page)

Apply

Example: The president of a successful computer software company wants to add a line of educational software. In order to do so, he must decide how many new programmers to hire and how many new salesmen. How would he use marginal analysis to make the decision?

Use something you have learned to solve a problem. Application questions require you to use more than one action. To answer the question above, you must do the following:

1. Define marginal analysis.

2. Describe the process of doing marginal analysis.

3. Apply marginal analysis to deciding how many programmers to hire *and* how many salesmen to hire.

Another wording: How could marginal analysis be used to decide how many computer programmers and how many salesmen to hire for a new business?

PREWRITING

In the exercises below you will practice strategies for taking tests. You will practice understanding the test question in Exercise 1. In Exercise 2 you will practice anticipating important terms and ideas. In Exercise 3 you will preview the test before you begin answering the questions.

Exercise 1: Understanding the Test Question

**Read the questions below. Underline the content words—
what you must write about. Then write the name of the type
of question. Use the chart on pages 81–82, "Types of Test
Questions," to help you. When you have finished, compare
your results with those of your classmates. (You do not have
to answer the questions.)**

1. What is marginal analysis?

2. What is the difference between a command economic system and a market economic system?

3. What is marginal analysis? How might the librarian at your school use marginal analysis to determine the hours the library stays open?

4. How does the elasticity of demand affect pricing?

5. Describe the two methods of measuring GNP.

6. How does a traditional economic system solve the economic problem? Give an example.

7. Explain how you would apply the concept of opportunity cost to deciding how long to study for an examination in a course where you hoped to get an "A." Would the opportunity costs be different if you were doing badly in the course? How?

8. You are a famous economics professor. The President of the United States phones you to ask whether her administration should follow the Keynesians or the supply-siders in order to keep the economy healthy. Which economic theory would you tell her to follow? Defend your position.

Exercise 2: *Anticipating Important Terms and Ideas*

When instructors write test questions, they try to ask about the most important terms or ideas. A good way to study for a test is to pretend *you* are the instructor and try to identify which terms and ideas are most important. For this exercise, assume you are writing a test on the reading selections in this unit.

A. List four or five important terms the students need to understand. Write test questions that require them to define the terms. Use the chart on page 81 to help you.

B. Think about the main idea and most important points of "Scarcity and Choice" and of "Making Choices." Then write three questions about each selection.

C. Work in pairs or small groups and read the questions you wrote. Identify the type and the content of each question. Then discuss how to answer it.

Exercise 3: *Previewing the Test*

Turn to the Economics Test on page 85. This is the test you are going to take in this unit. Read the questions and identify the question type and the content.

THE FIRST DRAFT

Taking the Test

CONTENT

Answer the questions on the economics test that follows. You may have as much time to finish as you need. You may use your book and your notes.

AUDIENCE

Your audience is your instructor. Your goal in writing the answers is to convince your instructor that you understand the basic economic principles you have been studying. As a result, be sure to explain everything fully. Summarize important ideas and define terms when necessary.

PROCEDURE

Here are some strategies for taking tests that will help you work most efficiently toward a good grade. Use these strategies when you take the economics test.

- Read the whole test first. Note how many points or what percentage each question counts and plan your time accordingly. Spend the most time on the questions that count the most.

- Analyze the questions. Be sure you understand what the question asks you to do and what the content words are so that you will answer the questions correctly and completely.

- Stop to think a minute before you answer a question. Plan your answer and, if possible, make a few notes to organize your answer. Use prewriting to help you get ideas and organize them. Write a thesis statement or topic sentence which gives a general answer to the question. Then support your generalizations with the concrete facts, examples, and information you learned from your reading and from class discussions.

- Work first on the questions you know the answers to or can answer most quickly and easily. If you cannot answer a question, move on to one you *can* answer. If you have time at the end of the test, go back to the questions that gave you trouble.

- When you are taking a test, especially a timed test, it is important not to rush. Take a few minutes to read over the test and plan your time. If a question counts only 10 percent of the total points possible, do not spend 25 percent of your time on it. In addition, leave yourself time at the end of the test to read over your answers. You may need to add something important, to delete something, correct your spelling, and so forth.

Economics Test

1. Briefly, identify the following. (20%)
   a. The economic problem
   b. The three basic questions
   c. Opportunity costs
   d. Marginal analysis

2. What are the productive resources? Briefly, discuss the role of each in an economic system and give examples. (40%)

3. Choose one of the following situations. (40%)
   a. You are ruler of a small island in the Pacific. Your island is poor and your people are not well educated. You do not manufacture anything the world wants nor do you have important crops or minerals to export. As the ruler, you are interested in bringing prosperity to your island. It is a beautiful island with a perfect climate, peaceful beaches, and wonderful places for swimming and boating. In addition, your people are attractive and friendly and welcome strangers. You decide that tourism will be your main industry, so you use your resources to build hotels. You advertise the island as a "Pacific Paradise." Evaluate this decision. In answering the question, consider how well you used the productive resources of your island, how you answered the three basic questions, and what the opportunity costs of your decision are.

   b. You are the "donut king" of your state. You own donut shops all over your state and they are doing well. Every shop you open makes a big profit and people seem to love your donuts. However, now frozen yogurt is becoming popular. There are not many frozen yogurt shops in your state yet, but in other states frozen yogurt shops are very profitable. You want your business to grow, but you can't decide whether to open more donut shops or to begin selling frozen yogurt in the shops you already own. If you open more donut shops, you will have to buy new shops and hire more salespeople. In addition, you will need more delivery trucks and more drivers. If you use the shops you already own to sell yogurt and donuts, you will not need new shops, salespeople, trucks or drivers, but you will need to buy and install the yogurt making machinery. How would marginal analysis and a consideration of opportunity costs help you make your decision?

THE SECOND DRAFT

In a real test, you do not have the opportunity to revise your answers to get a better grade. However, in this unit you are learning how to write better test answers, so you do have a chance to revise.

Learning about Writing

Before you turn in your test answers do the exercises below.

Exercise 1: Using Topic Sentences and Specific Details in Answers

You have already learned to use topic sentences and thesis statements when you write an essay. When you take a test, using topic sentences for short answers or thesis statements for longer answers will help you organize your answer. The topic sentence or thesis statement provides a very general answer to the question. Then you use specific examples to support the general statement.

A. Below is one student's answer to question 2 on the economics test. Reread question 2. Work in pairs or small groups. Decide what type of question it is and identify the content. Then read what the student wrote and answer the questions that follow.

Student Answer

Four kinds of productive resources—land, capital, labor, and management—are used in the production of goods. Land includes all kinds of natural resources, such as oil, water, minerals, fertile land, and even sunshine and rain. Capital refers to all manufactured resources such as the machinery and tools that are used to produce goods. Labor is the human resource, the manpower that uses machines to turn natural resources into goods. Finally, management is the ability to organize production and the creative ability to develop and invent new ways of doing things.

1. What is the topic sentence? Does it give a general answer to all of the content in the question? To part of the content? To none of the content?

2. What details support the topic sentence? How are they related to the content words of the question?

3. Did the writer answer the question completely? If not, what additional information would you include?

B. Here are some possible test questions on the material in this unit. For each question, write a topic sentence that is a general answer to the question.

1. What does an economist mean when he speaks of land as a productive resource?

2. What are the opportunity costs of going to college?

3. Explain how a college student who only wants a grade of "C" in a class might use marginal analysis to decide how much time to spend on studying for that class.

C. Now look at your own answers on the economics test. Did each answer begin with a topic sentence which gives a general answer to the question? If not, add topic sentences now.

Exercise 2: Using Summaries and Definitions in Answers

Defining terms and summarizing are very important when you take a test. For example, suppose a question asks you to evaluate the importance of capital and management as productive resources. Before you evaluate them, you must define *capital* and *management*.

A. Look again at the test question and answer in part A of Exercise 1 on page 86. The question asks the student to *discuss* the four kinds of resources. What else did the writer do when she answered the question?

B. Now look at your own answers on the economics test. Answer the questions below and add any missing definitions and summaries to your answers.

1. In your answer to question 2 did you briefly define your terms and summarize the important features of each kind of productive resource? If not, add definitions and summaries now.

2. If you answered question 3a, did you define productive resources and summarize what your book said about them? Did you summarize what the selection said about the three basic questions? Did you define opportunity costs? If not, add definitions and summaries now.

3. If you answered question 3b, did you define marginal analysis and opportunity costs? If not, add definitions now.

Exercise 3: Prewriting to Plan Your Answers

Whenever you take a test, you should take a minute to plan your answer before beginning to write. Prewriting techniques such as brainstorming and grouping can help you plan. Do the activities below to practice planning answers to test questions.

1. Look again at the questions and topic sentences you wrote for Exercise 1B on page 86. Pretend you are taking a test and decide which question you want to answer. Use some prewriting techniques to help you get ideas and plan your answer.

2. Now use the plan you just made to write an answer to the question. Begin with the topic sentence you wrote for Exercise 1B or write a new topic sentence. Then follow the plan to complete your answer.

3. Look at your answers to questions 2 and 3 on the economics test. Did you plan your answers? If you think you could improve any answers, use prewriting techniques to help you get ideas and plan. Then rewrite your answer.

Writing the Second Draft

You have made some important changes in your answers on the economics test, but there are probably some things you could do to improve it even more. Read your answers again and use the questions below to help you decide what other changes to make.

- Did you do what the question asked you to do: define, discuss, compare, etc?
- Is your answer complete? Did you include all the content?
- Did you define your terms?
- Did you summarize important ideas when necessary?
- Are your answers well organized? Did you start with a topic sentence and support it with details from your reading, notes, and class discussion?

Make whatever changes you need in order to answer the test questions completely and correctly.

Writing the Final Copy

When you are finished revising, edit your test answers for spelling, grammar, and punctuation. Copy your revised answers on clean paper.

Just for fun, grade your own test. To grade your test, look at your answers to the questions in Writing the Second Draft above. Count the number of *yeses*. Then use this grading scale:

Can answer *yes* to all questions	A
Can answer *yes* to most questions	B
Can answer *yes* to one-half to three-quarters of the questions	C
Can answer *yes* to one-quarter of the questions	D
Can answer *yes* to fewer than one-quarter of the questions	F

Write your grade on a separate piece of paper. When your instructor returns the test, compare your grade to your instructor's. How close were you to the grade the instructor wrote?

UNIT SIX
EXPRESSING AN OPINION

Business

In this unit you are going to read about working and about what makes work satisfying to people. You will read what two people have to say about their work. Then you will read about changes in what people want from work. Your writing assignment is to write a paper in which you state an opinion about the rewards of work and what makes work satisfying.

GETTING READY TO WRITE

Before you read the selections in this unit explore your own ideas about work. Think about work and the kind of job you would like. Then write down some ideas that you associate with work and jobs. You might begin like this:

- Work is like . . .
- Work involves . . .
- I would like a job in which I . . .
- A good job is one in which . . .

I. What Makes Work Satisfying?

The two selections that follow are taken from *Working* by Studs Terkel. Terkel is an oral historian. He asks people to talk about various topics. Then he tape-records what they say. He asked the two people below to talk about their work and how they felt about it. You will read their actual words, transcribed from the tape recording.

Before you read, discuss these questions with your classmates:

1. Why do people work?

2. Besides money, what else do people get from their work?

BABE SECOLI

Babe Secoli had been a checker at a supermarket for almost thirty years when Studs Terkel interviewed her. Here is what she had to say about her work:

"I started at twelve—a little, privately owned grocery store across the street from the house. They didn't have no cash registers. I used to mark the prices down on a paper bag.

"When I got out of high school, I didn't want no secretary job. I wanted the grocery job. It was so interesting for a young girl. I just fell into it. I don't know no other work but this. It's hard work, but I like it. This is my life. . . ."

You sort of memorize the prices. It just comes to you. I know half a gallon of milk is sixty-four cents; a gallon, $1.10. You look at the labels. . . . You just memorize. On the register is a list of some prices, that's for the part-time girls. I never look at it.

I don't have to look at the keys on my register. I'm like the secretary that knows her typewriter. The touch. My hand fits. The number nine is my big middle finger. The thumb is number one, two and three and up. The side of my hand uses the bar for the total and all that. . . .

I'm eight hours a day on my feet. It's just a physical tire of standing up. When I get home I get my second wind. . . .

My feet, they hurt at times, very much so. When I was eighteen years old I put the bathing suit on and I could see the map on my leg. From standing, standing. And not the proper shoes. So I wear like a nurse's shoes with good inner sole arch support, like Dr. Scholl's. They ease the pain and that's it. Sometimes I go to bed, I'm so tired that I can't sleep. My feet hurt as if I'm standing while I'm in bed.

I love my job. I've got very nice bosses. I got a black manager and he's just beautiful. They don't bother you as long as you do your work. And the pay is terrific. I automatically get a raise because of the union. Retail Clerks. Right now I'm ready for retirement as far as the union goes. I have enough years. I'm as high up as I can go. I make $189 gross pay. When I retire I'll make close to five hundred dollars a month. This is because of the union. Full benefits. The business agents all know me by name. The young kids don't stop and think what good the union's done. . . .

I'm a checker and I'm very proud of it. There's some, they say, "A checker—ugh!" To me, it's like somebody being a teacher or a lawyer. I'm not ashamed that I wear a uniform and nurse's shoes and that I got varicose veins. I'm makin' an honest living. Whoever looks down on me, they're lower than I am. . . .

I wouldn't know how to go in a factory. I'd be like in a prison. Like this, I can look outside, see what the weather is like. I want a little fresh air, I walk out the front door, take a few sniffs of air, and come back in. I'm here forty-five minutes early every morning. I've never been late except for that big snowstorm. I never thought of any other work.

I'm a couple of days away, I'm very lonesome for this place. When I'm on a vacation, I can't wait to go, but two or three days away, I start to get fidgety. I can't stand around and do nothin'. I have to be busy at all times. I look forward to comin' to work. It's a great feelin'. I enjoy it somethin' terrible.

LARRY ROSS

Larry Ross had been a business consultant since 1968 when Studs Terkel interviewed him. Here is what he said about his work:

The corporation is a jungle. It's exciting. You're thrown in on your own and you're constantly battling to survive. When you learn to survive, the game is to become the conqueror, the leader. . . .

I started in the corporate world, oh gosh—'42. After kicking around in the Depression, having all kinds of jobs and no formal education, I wasn't equipped to become an engineer, a lawyer, or a doctor. Gravitated to selling. Now they call it marketing. I grew up in various corporations. I became the executive vice-president of a large corporation and then of an even larger one. Before I quit I became president and chief executive officer of another. All nationally known companies. . . .

The executive is a lonely animal in the jungle who doesn't have a friend. Business is related to life. I think in our everyday living we're lonely. I have only a wife to talk to, but beyond that . . . When I talked business to her, I don't know whether she understood me. But that was unimportant. What's important is that I was able to talk out loud and hear myself—which is the function I serve as a consultant.

The executive who calls me usually knows the answer to his problem. He just has to have somebody to talk to and hear his decision out loud. If it sounds good when he speaks it out loud, then it's pretty good. As he's talking, he may suddenly realize his errors and he corrects them out loud. That's a great benefit wives provide for executives. She's listening and you know she's on your side. She's not gonna hurt you. . . .

Why didn't I stay in the corporate structure? As a kid, living through the Depression, you always heard about the tycoons, the men of power, the men of industry. And you kind of dream that. Gee, these are supermen. These are the guys that have no feeling, aren't subject to human emotions, the insecurities that everybody else has. You get in the corporate structure, you find they all button their pants the same way everybody else does. They all got the same fears. . . .

When the individual reaches the vice presidency or he's general manager, you know he's an ambitious, dedicated guy who wants to get to the top. He isn't one of the gray people. He's one of the black-and-white vicious people—the leaders, the ones who stick out in the crowd.

As he struggles in this jungle, every position he's in, he's terribly lonely. He can't confide and talk with the guy working under him. He can't confide and talk to the man he's working for. To give vent to his feelings, his fears, and his insecurities, he'd expose himself. This goes all the way up the line until he gets to be president. The president *really* doesn't have anybody to talk to, because the vice presidents are waiting for him to die or make a mistake and get knocked off so they can get his job. . . .

Working—People Talk About What They Do All Day and How They Feel About What They Do by Studs Terkel. Copyright © 1972, 1974, by Studs Terkel. Reprinted by permission of Pantheon Books, a division of Random House, Inc., New York.

I work on a yearly retainer with a corporation. I spend, one, two, three days a month in various corporate structures. The key executives can talk to me and bounce things off me. The president may have a specific problem that I will investigate and come back to him with ideas. The reason I came into this work is that all my corporate life I was looking for somebody like me, somebody who's been there. Because there's no new problems in business today. There's just a different name for different problems that have been going on for years and years and years. Nobody's come up yet with a problem that isn't familiar. I've been there . . .

THINK AND DISCUSS

Think about the following questions. Then discuss them with your classmates.

1. What does Babe Secoli do? What skills and knowledge does her job require? Do you think she is good at her job?

2. What does Larry Ross do? What skills and knowledge does his job require? Do you think he is good at his job?

3. In every society, some occupations are considered more important and desirable than others. We call these "high status" occupations. Societies differ in which occupations they consider high status and which they do not. What kinds of work do *you* consider high status? Low status? How do your answers compare with those of your classmates?

4. Whose job do you think has higher status—Babe's or Larry's? Who do you think earns more money? What do Babe and Larry have to say about what they earn and the kind of status their jobs have?

WRITING WARM-UP

Write a few sentences describing what Babe or Larry like most about their jobs. Save what you write. You may want to use it later.

_____

_____

_____

_____

II. What Do People Want from Their Work?

This reading is from *Reinventing the Corporation* by John Naisbitt and Patricia Aburdene. It is about changes in work and in the workplace. In this selection, the authors discuss changes in what workers expect from their work.

Before you read "Reinventing Work," discuss the questions below with your classmates.

1. Do you think work is worth doing for its own sake, even if it is boring or hard?

2. What do you expect from your own job or from the job you plan to have someday?

3. What did your parents expect from their jobs?

4. What did your grandparents expect from their jobs?

5. Are your expectations different from your parents' or grandparents'? If so, in what ways?

REINVENTING WORK

There is a new ideal [sic] about work emerging in America today. For the first time, there is widespread expectation that work should be fulfilling—and that work should be fun.

Thirty years ago, that would have been an outrageous notion. And in the parts of corporate America still run according to industrial values, it still is. Nevertheless, people know intuitively that work ought to be fun and satisfying, even when it is not. . . .

For millions of baby boomers, this new ideal is not outrageous; it is natural. Affluent and extremely well educated, they grew up believing life should be fun—and work, too. Who put this strange notion into their heads?

Oddly enough, it was probably their own parents, who grew up in the Depression and toiled in the factories of industrial America. For the parents of the baby boom, work was quite possibly *not* fun. Determined that their children would have more education and more of everything, parents sacrificed for their children's sake. And succeeded in giving them what they had lacked.

But the [sic] education and affluence change people's expectations. Result: The "work should be fun" ethic has begun to displace the puritan ethic, which holds that work is honorable and valuable in and of itself, that work must have some drudgery attached.

That new value is becoming the dominant attitude in today's workplace. Some 40 percent of the work force has adopted (at least in part) the notion that work should be personally satisfying rather than valuable for its own sake, according to Stephen A. Zimney of Yankelovich, Skelly & White, the New York market research firm, which has studied people's attitudes toward work for the past thirteen years. . . .

Reinventing the Corporation—Transforming Your Job and Your Company for the New Information Society, by John Naisbitt and Patricia Aburdene.
Reprinted by permission of Warner Books/NY. Copyright © 1985 by Megatrends Ltd. All rights reserved.

The New Ideal: Self-Management

We are shifting the ideal of the model employee from one who carries out orders correctly to one who takes responsibility and initiative, monitors his or her own work, and uses managers and supervisors in their new roles of facilitators, teachers, and consultants.

Throughout corporate America, there is evidence that people are increasingly expected to manage themselves. . . .

Companies today do not have the time, the personnel, or the resources to monitor people carefully. People have to manage themselves. Besides, people perform better when they manage themselves. . . .

Self-Management: How Close Are We?

But how many of us know how to manage ourselves?

America's great strength is people, well educated, ethically diverse, still full of the incentive to achieve economic success.

Yet today, people seem confused about work.

We say we want to work hard, but we often work just hard enough to get by.

On the one hand:

- A 1980 Gallup poll showed that 88 percent of Americans want to "work hard and to do the best on the job."
- More than half of the people interviewed for a 1983 Public Agenda Foundation study coauthored by Daniel Yankelovich of the research firm of Yankelovich, Skelly and White said that they have an inner need to do the very best job regardless of pay.

On the other hand:

- Half of the same people said they worked just hard enough to avoid getting fired.
- Seventy-five percent said they could be "significantly more effective on the job."

When asked why they do not work hard, they had two answers: (1) They do not get paid any more for working harder, and (2) managers provide little incentive to work hard.

Are people confused about work or is the workplace confused about people? It is becoming clearer and clearer that it is the workplace that is out of step with today's workers.

People want the satisfaction of knowing that their work is competent, respected, and effective. The vast majority of our workplaces are not structured to offer that satisfaction. What do people want in a job?

The 1983 Public Agenda Foundation study came up with these top ten qualities people want in a job today:

1. work with people who treat me with respect
2. interesting work
3. recognition for good work
4. chance to develop skills
5. working for people who listen if you have ideas about how to do things better
6. a chance to think for myself rather than just carry out instructions

7. seeing the end results of my work
8. working for efficient managers
9. a job that is not too easy
10. feeling well informed about what is going on

Notice that job security, high pay, and good benefits are not even on the top ten list (they made the top fifteen, though). Yet most companies deal with people as if security, pay, and benefits were the only ways to motivate them.

That is ironic, since these psychic rewards people want—challenging work, personal growth, learning new skills, autonomy, participation, respect, acknowledgment, effective management, and information—are exactly what business needs now.

If people did not already want these things, business would have to find a way to sell them these ideas, because these are the qualities corporations need to flourish in the new information era.

THINK AND DISCUSS

Think about the questions below. Then discuss them with your classmates.

1. The authors state that the puritan ethic has been replaced by the "work is fun" ethic. What is the puritan ethic? How does it differ from the "work is fun" ethic?

2. What do the authors mean above when they talk about the "psychic rewards" of work? What are some of those psychic rewards?

3. Explain how each of the following is important in making workers feel satisfied with their jobs. If you do not know what the expressions mean, try to use clues to their meanings from the reading itself. If you still do not know what the expressions mean, use your dictionary.

   - self-management
   - job security
   - employee benefits
   - challenge
   - autonomy
   - respect

4. What five or six things are most important to you in a job? Have someone list the responses of the class on the board. Then, as a group, decide which ten rewards are the most important. Compare the class's list with the list from the Public Agenda Foundation on page 94. How are the two lists similar? How are they different? If there are differences, how do you explain the differences? Copy the class list and save it. You will use it later.

WRITING WARM-UP

Write a few sentences in which you discuss the psychic rewards of work. If you have trouble getting started, you might complete this thought:

There are many things besides money which reward people for work. They include . . .

_____

_____

_____

_____

PREWRITING

When you write your essay, you will state your opinion about the rewards of work and what makes it satisfying. In order to make your essay convincing to your reader, you must support your opinion with specific details about people's attitudes about work. The exercise below will help you identify specific examples to use in your essay.

1. Review what Babe and Larry said about their work. Then list what they like and do not like on a form similar to the one below. Use a new form for each person, and be sure to write the name and occupation on the form.

What People Like/Don't Like about Their Jobs

Name _____ Occupation _____

Like

_____

_____

_____

Dislike

_____

_____

_____

---

2. Now do what Studs Terkel did and interview people about their jobs. Choose two people who have different jobs (a waitress and a teacher, for example). Ask them to talk to you for a few minutes about what they like and don't like about their jobs. Record what they say on a form as you did for Babe and Larry. Keep the forms. You will use them later.

THE FIRST DRAFT
Learning about Writing I

By now you have a great deal of *specific* information about what people like and dislike about their jobs. Before you write a first draft, however, you must identify the *general* rewards and satisfactions these specific likes and dislikes represent. The exercises below will give you practice in making generalizations about specific details.

Exercise 1: Identifying General Rewards and Satisfactions

Below are groups of statements about work. Notice that each group includes both things people like and things they don't like. Read the statements in each group. Then decide what *general* reward or satisfaction each group represents. Write the general reward or satisfaction on the line below each group. When you are finished, compare your work with a partner's. The reward for the first group has been identified for you.

1. They're always watching us; they don't trust us.
Sometimes I come in early; sometimes I stay late. My boss doesn't care as long as I get the work done.
I'm supposed to ask my supervisor's permission, even to go get a drink of water.
We don't have to punch a time clock. They know we'll put in a full day of work.

feeling trusted

2. My work is boring.
I just do the same thing over and over.
You have to think all the time in my job.
I do lots of different things at work.

_____

3. The company paid for me to take accounting classes.
I wanted to try putting the report on the computer, but they made me do it the old way instead.
I wanted to be production manager. I know I could have learned the job, but they hired someone who was already trained.
I've learned more about managing from my boss than you could ever learn from a book.

4. I wish my company would pay for child care instead of giving me all
that life insurance.
We only get a one-week vacation!
My company has really good health insurance.
The company sponsors exercise classes for employees.

Exercise 2: Organizing Your Details and Identifying General Rewards

You have read several selections about work and people's attitudes towards their
work. You have also interviewed people and discussed your own ideas with
your classmates. Now you need to analyze the specific details you have gathered
to generalize about job satisfaction and the rewards of work.

**Follow these steps to identify rewards and organize your
specific details.**

1. Review all your notes. As you look at all the specific details in your
   notes, what general rewards can you identify? Write the name of each
   reward at the top of a clean sheet of paper.

2. Below the name of each reward, list as many specific details and examples from your notes as you can.

3. Now rank the rewards.

   a. Which ones did most people mention? Write "most important" at the
   top of these sheets.

   b. Which ones seemed least important to people? Write "not important"
   at the top of those sheets.

   c. Are there any rewards that *you* think are important for which you
   don't have a sheet of paper? If so, write the name of that reward on
   another sheet of paper. What specific details or examples of this
   reward can you think of? List them on the sheet.

Exercise 3: Developing a Thesis

**Now look at the rewards you have identified. What kinds of
rewards seem most important to people? What kinds of
rewards seem least important? Use this information to write
a thesis statement in which you generalize about what makes
work satisfying.**

Writing the First Draft

CONTENT

Write the first draft of an essay in which you state an opinion about the rewards
of work. Remember that the purpose of a first draft is to get your ideas down
on paper. A first draft is never perfect or complete.

AUDIENCE

Your audience is your instructor and the other students in the class. Even though they have read the material and participated in class discussions, your opinion about what makes work satisfying may differ from those of your classmates. Your job in this assignment is to convince your readers that *your* opinion is valid. In order to convince them, you must state the rewards you think are most important and support your statements with specific details that show why those rewards are important.

PROCEDURE

- Use the sheets you developed in Exercise 2 on page 98 to organize the body of your essay. Omit any rewards you do not think are important.

- Plan which reward you will discuss first, second, third, etc. Arrange your sheets in the order in which you will use them.

- Read over the thesis statement you wrote in Exercise 3 on page 98. Does it generalize about *all* the rewards you plan to discuss? If not, revise your thesis statement.

- Write at least one paragraph about each reward. Your paragraph should have a topic sentence, which is supported with specific details from your reading, from your interviews, and from class discussion.

- Write an introduction to your essay that includes the thesis statement. You do not need to write the introduction first. Writers often write an introduction after they have written the rest of their essays. Your introduction might include statements about what is not important for job satisfaction or about where you got your information or about why it is important to understand the kinds of rewards people want from their work.

- Write a conclusion that either sums up what you have said, makes a prediction about the future, or recommends changes in how employers treat employees.

THE SECOND DRAFT

When you have written your first draft, put it away for a day or so before you revise.

Learning about Writing II

RELATIONSHIPS BETWEEN SENTENCES IN A PARAGRAPH

In a paragraph, the support sentences are not only related to the topic sentence, but they are related to each other as well. Good writers do not make their readers guess what these relationships are. They use words and phrases like *but*, *because*, and *for example* to show the relationship.

Read the sentences below:

- Raul makes good money at ABC Corporation.
- Raul would like to be given more challenging work assignments.

How are these sentences related? Does Raul feel he should be given more challenging assignments *because* he makes good money and thinks he should really earn it? Or is Raul unhappy *even though* he makes good money, because the assignments are not challenging? Unless the two ideas are linked with words and phrases like *because* or *even though*, the reader cannot fully understand what the writer means.

In the following exercises you will practice using words and phrases to show the relationships between ideas.

Exercise 1: Showing Relationships between Ideas

Read the pairs of ideas below. Then see how many different kinds of relationships you can show. Use the table on page 101 to help you. You may have to change the tense of the verb, add words, make the verb negative, etc. The first one is done for you.

1. David . . . be rude to his boss
   David . . . get fired

   Because David was rude to his boss, he got fired.
   After David was rude to his boss, he got fired.
   If David is rude to his boss, he will get fired.
   Although David was rude to his boss, he did not get fired.

2. Maria . . . hate her job
   Maria . . . earn a good salary

3. Workers . . . be respected
   Workers . . . be satisfied with their jobs

4. New kind of workers . . . think work should be fun
   Workplace . . . change

5. Sarah . . . need more money
   Sarah . . . get a new job

Words and Phrases That Show Relationships

On the left is a list of some of the ways ideas may be related. On the right is a list of some words and phrases which show that relationship.

addition	and, too, also, in addition, furthermore, not only . . . but also
cause/effect	so, because, as a result
choice	or, either . . . or
concession	although, even though
condition	if, unless
contrast	but, however, on the other hand
emphasis	indeed, oddly enough, in fact
explanation/example	for example, in other words
purpose	so that, in order to
reference	it, they, this, that, these, those
sequence	first, second, next, finally
time	when, after, before, as soon as

Exercise 2: Identifying Relationships in a Paragraph

Read the paragraph below about Babe Secoli. Then answer the questions that follow.

In some cases, the underlined word or phrase shows the relationship between two clauses or sentences. Other underlined words or phrases show how the idea that follows is related to the topic sentence.

Some people think being a supermarket checker would be boring and not very rewarding, but not Babe Secoli. She loves her job <u>and</u> is proud of the work
she does. One of the most important things to Babe is that she is very good at her job. She knows the prices and knows the keys on her register. <u>That</u> makes her very fast, <u>so</u> people want her to check them out. The working conditions are good, <u>too</u>. Her boss is nice and doesn't interfere with her <u>but</u> lets her do her own work, and she is free to step outside for fresh air when she wants. The last thing Babe mentions is the pay and security. <u>They</u> are important to her, too. She just got a raise because she belongs to the union, and she can retire with a pension anytime she wants. <u>Because</u> <u>it</u> holds satisfaction for her, Babe doesn't feel that her job is low status. She says it is "honest work," <u>and</u> she feels good about doing it.

1. Which sentence is the topic sentence of the paragraph?

2. The paragraph discusses Babe's feelings about her job. How many times does the writer repeat the word *job* to relate it to the topic? How many times does the writer use a pronoun for *job* to relate it to the topic?

3. Identify what relationship between ideas the underlined words in the paragraph show. Write the relationship on the lines by the words below. The words are numbered in the order in which they occur in the paragraph. The first relationship is identified for you.

(1) and *addition*

(6) They _____

(2) That _____

(7) Because _____

(3) so _____

(8) it _____

(4) too _____

(9) and _____

(5) but _____

Exercise 3: *Improving a Paragraph by Making Relationships Clear*

In the paragraph below all the words and phrases that show relationships have been removed. Rewrite the paragraph to show how the ideas are related and make it read smoothly.

You may combine sentences, use pronouns, change the form of the verb and change word order as necessary. Before you begin, you may want to reread the interview with Larry Ross on page 91. When you are finished, compare your paragraph with the paragraphs your classmates wrote. Were they all the same, or were there several different ways of relating the ideas?

   Larry Ross was a highly paid business consultant. It was not the money which made his work satisfying. He wasn't interested in having power or status in his job. He would have remained a business executive. Larry's real satisfactions at work came from helping and teaching others. He enjoyed sharing his knowledge with an executive who needed help in solving a problem. He got satisfaction from teaching young salesmen. He enjoyed watching young salesmen become real leaders in their companies. Larry liked helping executives. He compared himself to a psychiatrist. He said the most important thing he did was listen to the executives. The executives were lonely in their jobs. The executives had no one to whom they could talk safely. The satisfaction of doing his job well was important to Larry. He really knew what the problems were and how to solve them.

RELATIONSHIPS IN LONGER PIECES OF WRITING

Ideas in an essay are related at all levels: sentences are related to each other, sentences in a paragraph are related to the topic sentence, and paragraphs are related to the thesis. The exercises below will help you understand how to make the relationships in your essay clear to your reader.

Exercise 4: Relating Paragraphs to the Thesis

One way writers show the relationship between paragraphs and the thesis is to repeat key words or phrases from the thesis. The thesis of "The Stages of Adjustment" in Unit One is that people who travel or live in foreign countries go through stages of adjustment. What words or phrases do you think the writer of the selection will repeat in the body paragraphs?

Turn to the selection on page 3 and read the first sentence of each body paragraph. List the words or phrases that are repeated frequently.

Exercise 5: Relating Paragraphs to Each Other

It is also important to show how the body paragraphs in an essay are related to each other. When you start a new paragraph in an essay, your reader needs to know whether you are changing the topic, adding more information about the same topic, contrasting the information in two paragraphs, showing order in a sequence, and so on. Sometimes a single word such as *first, next,* or *finally* can show the relationship between paragraphs. At other times, writers need phrases or even whole sentences to indicate the relationship.

The paragraphs below are taken from "The Stages of Adjustment" in Unit One. The paragraphs discuss the fourth and the fifth stages of adjustment.

Read the thesis statement and the paragraphs. Then answer the questions. The paragraphs have been numbered for this exercise.

Thesis statement: Someone who goes to stay in a foreign country, whether it is for a short time or forever, passes through several stages of adjusting to the newness of the culture.

(1) *By the fourth stage* the travelers are functioning well. The language is no longer the struggle it once was. The currency is no longer unfamiliar. They know what to expect and how to get what they want.

(2) And just at *this time* a strange thing happens. They begin to feel more alienated than they did when they first arrived. Though life has become easier and they are coping well, they become irritable. Some become depressed. What they once found exciting and interesting in the new country is now annoying or hateful. They no longer want

to go out and explore their new surroundings. They withdraw into themselves. They are experiencing the classic symptoms of culture shock.

(3) *What has happened* is that by adjusting to their new surroundings, they lose the sense of self. In giving up a little of their old culture and taking on some of the new, the very foundations of their identity are threatened. It is a frightening experience, and they cope with their fear by withdrawing from the new culture and temporarily retreating back to being spectators. Some even find that they can no longer use the new language as well as they had only days or weeks before.

(4) *This stage*, the culture shock stage, may be long or short, depending on the individual. Eventually, though, the travelers begin participating again in the culture and they find to their amazement that they no longer feel so foreign. Out of the depression and sense of loss they experienced in the fourth stage comes real adjustment to the new land. They are less excited than they were in stage two, but their experiences are no longer a blur of heightened emotions and senses. They participate more than they did in stage three, but with less effort. In short, they have adapted to and become a part of their new country.

(5) *The final stage*, the re-entry stage, occurs when or if the travelers return to their native lands. When they do, they find that they are not quite the same people as they were when they left. They have changed. Their values are broader and more flexible. They have learned new and often better ways of being and thinking. Their friends and family seem slightly narrow and inflexible. Worse, their friends and family are only mildly interested in the exciting things that happened to them during their sojourn abroad. To their amazement, they feel just a little bit foreign in their own homeland.

1. Read the thesis statement. Which words in the thesis do the italicized words in paragraph 1 refer to?

2. What does *this time* tell you about the relationship between paragraph 1 and paragraph 2?

3. By using the phrase *what has happened*, is the writer telling you that paragraph 3 will discuss another stage of adjustment, that paragraph 3 explains more about the topic of paragraph 2, or that paragraph 3 is related to the thesis because it tells what happens to travelers in foreign countries?

4. How is paragraph 4 related to paragraphs 1, 2, and 3? What word or phrase tells you it is related?

5. Which of the following does the phrase *The final stage* in paragraph 5 tell you?

    a. This paragraph discusses the last stage in a sequence.

    b. This paragraph introduces a new topic—another stage of adjustment.

    c. This paragraph is related to the thesis because it discusses one of the stages of adjustment travelers go through.

    d. All of the above.

    e. None of the above.

Exercise 6: *Showing Relationships in Your Own Essay*

Work with a partner and exchange first drafts. Read your partner's essay two times.

A. The first time you read your partner's essay, ask yourself the questions below. If any of the relationships are not clear, question your partner.

1. How is each paragraph related to the one before it?

2. Are the relationships between paragraphs clear?

    a. If they are, how has my partner shown the relationships?

    b. If not, what can my partner do to make the relationships clear?

B. The second time you read, look at the relationships within the paragraphs and ask yourself the questions below about the sentences in each paragraph. If any of the relationships are not clear, question your partner.

1. How is the sentence related to the topic sentence or to the sentence before it?

2. Is the relationship clear?

    a. If it is, how has my partner shown the relationship?

    b. If not, what can my partner do to make the relationship clear?

When you are finished, return the essay to your partner and suggest how it can be improved.

Writing the Second Draft

You have made some important changes in your essay. But there are probably some things you could do to improve it even more. Read your essay again and use the questions below to help you decide what additional changes to make.

- Is the thesis clear? Does it generalize about *all* the rewards discussed?
- Does each paragraph have a single topic that all the details support?
- Are the relationships between ideas in the paragraphs clear?
- Are the relationships between the paragraphs and the thesis clear?

Make whatever changes you need to express and support your opinion and make the relationships between the ideas in your essay clear to your reader.

Writing the Final Copy

When you are finished revising, edit your essay for errors in spelling, grammar, and punctuation. If you have not already given your essay a title, add one now. Copy your revised draft neatly on clean paper before you hand it in to your instructor.

UNIT SEVEN
TAKING A POSITION

History, Law, and Political Science

In this unit you are going to read selections from the fields of history, law, and political science. You will be reading a part of the Constitution of the United States, called the Bill of Rights, which guarantees basic freedoms to American citizens. You will also read parts of actual cases that were brought before the Supreme Court of the United States. These cases will help prepare you for the unit assignment in which you will act as a judge, take a position on how to apply the law, and write an opinion.

GETTING READY TO WRITE

I. The Bill of Rights

When the U.S. Constitution was written in 1787, many citizens felt that it had a major flaw because it did not name the specific rights for which the American Revolution was fought. The writers had thought that everyone would know that these principles were the foundation of the document, but those who had risked their lives for these freedoms demanded that they appear in written form. Americans did not want to trust their newly won liberties to the short memory of governments. In order to win approval for the new Constitution, the ten rights that the people considered most important were included as the first ten amendments. These amendments are known as the Bill of Rights.

Before you read the Bill of Rights and the case studies that follow, discuss these questions with your classmates.

1. What words or phrases come to mind when you hear the word freedom?

2. Why is freedom so important?

3. Which of these freedoms is the most important to you? Describe an experience you have had or have read about that illustrates the importance of this freedom.

   • freedom of speech
   • freedom to run your own business

- freedom to hold political meetings
- freedom of religion
- freedom of the press
- freedom to study

4. Below are three ways to begin a definition of freedom. Complete each one, using more than one sentence if necessary. If you use an example, introduce it with the words "for instance" or "for example."

- Freedom is a concept that involves . . .
- The word *freedom* can mean . . .
- Freedom means . . .

The Bill of Rights is divided into sections called Articles.
Read the ten articles; then reread Article 1, which you will
be analyzing in this unit.

THE BILL OF RIGHTS

Article 1

Congress shall make no law respecting an establishment of religion, or prohibiting the free exercise thereof or abridging the freedom of speech, or of the press; or the right of the people to peaceably assemble, and to petition the government for a redress of grievances.

Article 2

A well-regulated militia being necessary to the security of a free State, the right of the people to keep and bear arms shall not be infringed.

Article 3

No soldier shall, in time of peace, be quartered in any house, without the consent of the owner, nor in time of war but in a manner prescribed by law.

Article 4

The right of the people to be secure in their persons, houses, papers, and effects, against unreasonable searches and seizures, shall not be violated, and no warrants shall issue, but upon probable cause, supported by oath and affirmation, and particularly describing the place to be searched, and the person or things to be seized.

Article 5

No person shall be held to answer for capital, or otherwise infamous crime, unless on a presentment or indictment of a Grand Jury, except in cases arising in the land or naval forces, or in the militia, when in actual service in time of war or public danger; nor shall any person be subject for the same offense to be twice put in jeopardy of life or limb; nor shall be compelled in any criminal case to be a witness against himself; nor be deprived of life, liberty, or property, without due process of law; nor shall private property be taken for public use, without just compensation.

Article 6

In all criminal prosecutions the accused shall enjoy the right to a speedy and public trial, by an impartial jury of the State and district wherein the crime shall have been committed, which district shall have been previously ascertained by law, and to be informed of the nature and cause of the accusation; to be confronted with witnesses against him; to have compulsory process for obtaining witnesses in his favor; and to have the assistance of counsel for his defense.

Article 7

In suits of common law, where the value of the controversy shall exceed twenty dollars, the right of trial by jury shall be preserved, and no fact tried by a jury shall be otherwise reexamined in any court of the United States, than according to the rules of common law.

Article 8

Excessive bail shall not be required, nor excessive fines imposed, nor cruel and unusual punishments inflicted.

Article 9

The enumeration in the Constitution of certain rights shall not be construed to deny or disparage others retained by the people.

Article 10

The powers not delegated to the United States by the Constitution, nor prohibited by it to the States, are reserved to the States respectively, or to the people.

THINK AND DISCUSS

Think about the following questions. Then discuss them with your classmates.

1. Legal prose of the eighteenth century tended to put everything into one long sentence. Today we might arrange these same items in a list. Complete the following list for Article 1 (usually referred to as the First Amendment).

Congress shall make no law

    respecting an establishment of religion

    prohibiting the free exercise of religion

    abridging the freedom of speech

    abridging _____

    abridging _____

    abridging _____

2. The word *respecting* can mean "concerning" or "honoring." Which meaning does it have in the First Amendment?

3. This amendment is the source for the American political doctrine known as "separation of church and state." According to this doctrine the First Amendment protects all religions because it does not recognize any one as a state religion. Are there disadvantages to living in a country with a single state religion? If so, what are some of the disadvantages?

4. Are atheists and agnostics protected by the First Amendment?

5. Does freedom of speech give a citizen the right to say exactly what he or she wants to say at any time at any place to anybody? Does this freedom extend to the written word as well? To art? To movies? To recordings? Can you think of a situation in which freedom of speech *should* be abridged?

6. Why is a free press important in a democracy? Can you think of an example from your own experience or from your reading that illustrates the importance of a free press?

7. The First Amendment gives American citizens the right to gather together in groups, meetings, conferences, or parades as long as they do so peacefully. Why is this an important right?

8. American citizens have the right to ask their government to correct a wrong done against individuals or groups by making new laws or enforcing old ones. Which phrase in the First Amendment gives them that right?

9. The First Amendment groups the following rights: freedom of religion, freedom of the press, freedom of speech, freedom of peaceable assembly, and freedom to petition the government. Why do you think these were grouped together? What do they have in common?

WRITING WARM-UP

In two or three sentences, explain one of the freedoms guaranteed in the First Amendment. To make your explanation clearer use examples from your own experience or from class discussion.

_____

_____

_____

II. Case Law

The Constitution, like any body of law, is words on paper until it is tested in court. In the U.S. legal system, opposing sides present their cases to a judge or a jury to decide. Each side explains its position, then supports it with reasons and facts. When a decision is reached, the losing side may choose to appeal to a higher court to have the decision overturned.

The following cases were brought before the Supreme Court of the United States, the highest court in the land and the court of final appeal. This court is made up of nine judges, called Justices, who are appointed for life. One of the Justices is designated as the Chief Justice. The Supreme Court can decide by a simple majority of 5 to 4 that a conviction or decision should be overturned ("be reversed") or left standing ("affirmed").

Before you read, discuss the following question. All of the cases you will read in this section involve the First Amendment. It is the subject of more Supreme Court cases than any other amendment. Why do you think that this is so?

CASE 1. FEINER v. NEW YORK, 1951*

Summary

Irving Feiner was convicted of disorderly conduct at an open-air meeting where he was the speaker. He was sentenced by New York State to thirty days in prison. Feiner appealed the conviction on the grounds that his right of free speech was violated.

Historical Background

The action for which Irving Feiner was arrested took place at the beginning of the cold war, the term used to describe the conflict between the Soviet Union and the United States after World War II. Although the superpowers did not face each other directly in a shooting war, the conflict produced war-like tensions in both countries. In the United States individuals who were known to be communists were considered suspicious; eventually, even people who were suspected of being communist were thought to be dangerous. Soon anyone who opposed the government for whatever reason was labeled a communist. This period of hysteria placed everyone's First Amendment rights in jeopardy.

*The titles of the cases used in this unit consist of four elements: the name of the defendant; *v.*, the abbreviation of the Latin word *versus*, meaning "against"; the name of the state where the case was prosecuted; the date the case was tried.

Facts

1. On March 8, 1949, Feiner stood on a wooden box and used a loudspeaker to urge his listeners to come to a meeting in the Syracuse Hotel in New York. In the course of the speech, he made insulting remarks about President Truman, the American Legion, and the mayor of Syracuse. He said, "Truman is a bum . . . the mayor is a bum."* Because there was a crowd of about seventy-five to eighty people, some pedestrians were forced to walk in the street to avoid the crowd.

2. At first the police were concerned only about the effect of the crowd on the traffic. Then the crowd became excited when Feiner urged that blacks should fight for their rights. Some listeners threatened violence if the police did not stop him. Others sided with the speaker. An officer asked Feiner to break up the crowd and to get down off his box. He continued. Once more the officer asked him to stop talking. The speaker continued. Then the officer put Feiner under arrest.

Opinions of Two Justices

Opinion 1. Chief Justice Vinson: ". . . The officers in making the arrest were motivated solely by a proper concern for the general welfare, and there was no evidence that the acts of the police were a cover for the suppression of the petitioner's views and opinions. [Feiner] was neither arrested nor convicted for the content of his speech. Rather, it was the reaction the speech engendered. . . . The conviction of [Feiner] for violation of the public peace does not exceed the bound of proper state police action."

Opinion 2. Mr. Justice Black: "The record before us convinces me that [Feiner] has been sentenced for the unpopular views he expressed on matters of public interest while lawfully making a streetcorner speech . . . I think this conviction makes a mockery of the free speech guarantee of the First Amendment. The end result is to approve a simple technique by which cities and states can subject all speech, political or otherwise, to the censorship of the local police. I will have no part or parcel in this holding, which I view as a long step toward totalitarian authority.

THINK AND DISCUSS

Think about the following questions. Then discuss them with your classmates.

1. Do citizens have the right to expect to live in peace? Does the state have the right to maintain public order? Which opinion considers that the right to keep the peace was a more important right in this case than the right of free speech?

2. Did Feiner have the right to say what he did? What gave him that right? Which opinion considers the right of free speech to be a more important right in this case than the right to keep the peace?

*Ellipses (. . .) indicate where text has been deleted.
Brackets ([ ]) indicate where the authors have added words to make the text easier to read.

3. Earlier free speech cases established the principle that there has to be a clear and present danger to public peace and order—for instance, that the speaker's words might convince people to riot—before the right of free speech can be overlooked. From the evidence presented, do you think that there was a clear and present danger of disturbance of the peace? Why or why not?

4. In your opinion, which right should be considered the more important in this case, the right to free speech or the right to public order? Why do you think so?

Decision

In *Feiner v. New York*, Chief Justice Vinson's position represented the view of the majority. Justice Black's decision represented the minority view. Feiner lost his appeal and the court affirmed his conviction.

WRITING WARM-UP

Do you agree or disagree with this decision? In a few sentences, state your position and explain why you chose it.

_____

_____

_____

_____

CASE 2. EDWARDS v. SOUTH CAROLINA, 1963

Summary

187 black high school and college students were convicted of breach of the peace in Columbia, South Carolina. They appealed the conviction on the grounds that their right to peaceable assembly under the First Amendment was violated.

Historical Background

The action for which the students were convicted took place at the beginning of the civil rights movement in America. Led by the Reverend Martin Luther King, Jr., this movement was characterized by its public commitment to nonviolence. Eventually, the movement succeeded in pressuring Congress and the President to pass and approve legislation enforcing civil rights for all Americans, whatever their race, creed, or color. The state where the student action took place was a state that practiced segregation by law—prohibiting blacks from eating in "white" restaurants, going to "white" public schools or colleges, and living in "white" parts of town.

Facts

1. On March 2, 1961, the petitioners [the black students] walked in small groups to the state house. Their purpose was to submit a protest against discrimination and to ask that laws enforcing segregation be removed. As they entered the state house grounds, they were told that they had every right to walk around the grounds as long as the group remained peaceful.

2. They walked in small groups around the grounds for the next half hour, some carrying placards that said "Down with segregation." There were about 200 onlookers, but traffic was not obstructed, nor were there any hostile gestures or words between the onlookers and the students.

3. Then the police warned the petitioners that they would be arrested if they didn't leave in fifteen minutes. Instead of leaving, they engaged in what the city manager called "loud" and "flamboyant conduct." Later testimony established that the conduct consisted of listening to a religious sermon and singing the national anthem while stamping their feet and clapping their hands. After fifteen minutes, the police arrested the petitioners.

Opinions of Two Justices

Opinion 1. Justice Stewart: ". . . the circumstances in this case reflect an exercise of these basic constitutional rights in their most pristine and classic form. The petitioners felt aggrieved by the laws of South Carolina . . . they peaceably assembled and peaceably expressed their grievances. Not until they were told to disperse on pain of arrest did they do more. Even then, they but sang patriotic and religious songs. There was no violence or threat of violence on their part or on the part of anyone watching . . . the opinions they were expressing were sufficiently opposed to the views of the majority of the community to attract a crowd and necessitate police protection . . . the Amendment does not permit a state to make criminal the peaceful expression of unpopular views."

Opinion 2. Justice Clark: "Petitioners had the right to peaceable assembly and to petition but in my view the manner in which they exercised their rights was by no means a passive demonstration . . . The question seems to me whether a State is constitutionally prohibited from enforcing breach of peace laws in a situation where the city officials believe that disorder and violence are imminent . . . In *Feiner v. New York* we upheld a conviction for breach of peace in a situation no more dangerous than that found here. There a demonstration was conducted by only one person and the crowd was limited to 80 people. There the petitioner was urging blacks to fight for equal rights; here 200 black demonstrators were being aroused to fever pitch before 300 people, some of whom were hostile. Perhaps their speech was not animated, but their placards read, "You may jail our bodies but not our souls" and they chanted

"I Shall Not Be Moved"* and stamped their feet and clapped their hands, creating a danger of riot. It is my belief that anyone [who knows small Southern towns] recognizes the danger of combustion . . . and will agree that the City Manager's action may well have averted a major catastrophe . . . to say that the police may not intervene until the riot has occurred is like keeping out the doctor until the patient dies."

THINK AND DISCUSS

Think about the following questions. Then discuss them with your classmates.

1. Justice Stewart states that in this case the right to peaceable assembly is a more important right than the right to public peace. Can one right be more important than another? Who should make that decision?

2. What does Justice Clark believe to be the more important right in this case? How does he justify his opinion?

3. There is a saying in law that reasonable people may disagree. Such disagreement is the basis of legal argument. For example, both justices use the same fact—that the demonstrators were stamping and clapping—to come to different conclusions. What are the different conclusions? How do you think each justice arrived at his separate conclusion?

4. Justice Clark used the *Feiner* case as a precedent to support his opinion. Precedents are cases that have already been decided. They are used to support an opinion. A good precedent is one that is very similar to the present case. In your opinion, is the *Feiner* case enough like the *Edwards* case to be a good precedent?

> **Decision**
>
> Justice Stewart's view was the majority view. Justice Clark's was the minority view. The students' conviction was overturned.

WRITING WARM-UP

Do you agree or disagree with this decision? In a few sentences, state your position and explain why you chose it.

_____

_____

_____

_____

*This is a folk song associated with the fight for union rights.

PREWRITING

Your assignment for this unit is to write an opinion about a First Amendment case. The report that follows is based on a real incident. The attorneys for the Aryan Party protested a court order on the grounds that the First Amendment right of peaceable assembly had been violated; however, they did not take the case to the Supreme Court because the concert was canceled due to bad weather.

Read the report.

On March 3, 1989, a California judge halted a weekend concert advertised as an "Aryan Woodstock"* that would feature racist rock-and-roll music by neo-Nazi bands from around the country. The concert was sponsored by a neo-Nazi organization known as the Aryan Party. Members of this neo-Nazi group are characterized by their close-cropped hair or shaved heads and their belief in the supremacy of the white race. These so-called "skinheads" have been linked to racially motivated murders and assaults around the country.

Ruling on the county's request for a restraining order or injunction, the judge decided that although the group had a permit, they could not hold the planned concert because "it would almost inevitably lead to violence."

Local and county officials had quickly organized to oppose the gathering as news of the concert began to spread. About 1400 law-enforcement officers from two counties were placed on alert to respond to any possible violence.

Concert organizers had presented themselves as members of an environmental action group when they leased the land from a local physician. When word got out that the concert was to feature such skinhead groups as the Bootboys and the Hammerheads, local civil rights organizations began their protest. The Jewish Defense League, the Anti-Klan League, and the Joint Conference of Christians and Jews to Fight Racism vowed to stop this concert by any means possible.

A tape-recorded message on a special telephone line called "Aryan Update" said the concert was for whites only and warned "all you race mixers to stay home." The neo-Nazi organizer of the event appeared before the county board of supervisors to argue that the only issue in the case was the right of free assembly.

Attorneys for the neo-Nazi group vowed to take it all the way to the Supreme Court.

*Woodstock was an outdoor rock concert that took place in Woodstock, New York, in the summer of 1969. It signaled the beginning of protest by young people against the establishment.

THINK AND DISCUSS

Think about the following questions. Then discuss them with your classmates.

1. Under the Constitution are all groups allowed to demonstrate or peaceably assemble?

2. Are the rights of the bystanders ignored if those with opposing views are permitted to demonstrate?

3. What is your initial reaction to this case? If you were the judge, would you grant the restraining order? Don't worry about making a final decision yet. You may find that you change your opinion as you examine the case more thoroughly.

THE FIRST DRAFT

Learning about Writing I

BUILDING AN ARGUMENT

American law has two foundations: written law and case law. Written law is the recorded laws of each state and the Constitution. Case law is the accumulation of all the decisions that judges and juries make. Each case that is decided becomes a precedent that can be used as part of a lawyer's argument or a judge's opinion.

Exercise 1. Choosing Statements for Precedents

Below are the opinions of two justices in another case, *Gregory v. Chicago*, 1969. In this case the Supreme Court overturned the conviction of demonstrators; their demonstration enraged onlookers so much that the police thought there would be a riot. To prevent a riot the demonstrators were arrested.

Read the facts and opinions and answer the questions that follow.

Facts

1. A group of demonstrators, accompanied by the Chicago police, marched in a peaceful and orderly procession to the mayor's residence to press their claim for desegregation of the public schools.

2. Although the demonstrators continued to be peaceful, the onlookers became unruly as the number of bystanders increased.

3. To prevent what they regarded as inevitable civil disorder, the Chicago police demanded, under threat of arrest, that the demonstrators disperse.

4. When this command was not obeyed, the demonstrators were arrested.

Two Opinions

Opinion 1. "Both police and demonstrators made their best efforts but . . . were unable to restrain the hostile hecklers within orderly bounds. These facts disclosed by the record point unerringly to one conclusion, namely, that when groups with diametrically opposed, deep-seated views are permitted to air their emotional grievances, side by side, on city streets, tranquility and order cannot be maintained even by the joint efforts of police and protesters."

Opinion 2. "When the policeman in charge of the special police detail concluded that the hecklers observing the march were dangerously close to rioting, and that the demonstrators were likely to be engulfed in that riot, he ordered Gregory and his demonstrators to leave and Gregory—standing on what he deemed to be his constitutional rights—refused to do so. To let a policeman's command become equivalent to a criminal statute comes dangerously close to making our government one of men rather than of law. . . . "

1. Imagine that you are a lawyer looking for a precedent in a First Amendment case being argued before the Supreme Court. You want the judges to overturn a conviction by police officers who have used force to stop a riot at an outdoor political rally. Which statement from *Gregory v. Chicago* would you use to support your request?

2. Now imagine that you are a lawyer looking for a precedent to support a request that the conviction by the police officers should be upheld. Which statement would you use?

Exercise 2. Reviewing Previous Cases for Precedents

Review all the cases you have studied so far, looking for precedents to support the position you have taken on the Aryan Party case. Make a list of the precedents.

Cite each source by using the title of the case and paraphrasing the relevant section. As you might expect, it is always better to use a precedent from the winning side.

Exercise 3. Identifying the Flow of an Argument

Arguments can be arranged in many different ways. One of the most common is to begin with a specific instance and then progress to a general statement; another way is to begin with the general statement and end with the most specific detail.

Read each argument below and decide in which order it is arranged.

1. A version of this argument was used in the Declaration of Independence, the document that helped start the American Revolution.

> The King has broken his word to us.
>
> He has refused to listen to our just complaints.
>
> We are burdened with new taxes even though we thought he understood that the old taxes were too high.

2. A version of this argument was used in an important Supreme Court decision before the American Civil War, which was fought over slavery and states' rights.

> In states where slavery is legal, a slave is the property of his master.
>
> The Constitution states that no one can be deprived of his rights or his property without due process.
>
> A man and his slave may leave a state where it is legal to keep slaves and travel to a state where slavery is illegal without putting himself in danger of automatically losing his property.
>
> The laws of one state cannot automatically overrule the laws of another state.

3. A version of this argument was used to extend the meaning of "free speech" to sign language.

> Freedom of speech means the freedom to communicate one's thoughts publicly.
>
> Individuals ordinarily communicate through speech, that is, words produced by the vocal cords.
>
> Deaf persons often communicate through sign language, which can be understood as a form of speech.

4. Reread the extracts from the opinions in *Edwards v. South Carolina* on page 114. In which order are they arranged?

Writing the First Draft

CONTENT

As a Supreme Court Justice, you have been asked to take a position and write an opinion in response to the following appeal:

> The neo-Nazi Party asks that the injunction against the Aryan Woodstock concert be overturned on the grounds that their rights for peaceable assembly were denied.

AUDIENCE

Your audience is the American people. You will need to use precedents and quotes from other cases to support your opinion.

PROCEDURE

- List the facts in the case.
- Form a preliminary opinion based on the facts.
- Reread the other First Amendment cases in this unit.
- Select statements from these cases that support your opinion.
- Decide how to arrange the statements in your argument.
- Use the following form when you draft your opinion.

Aryan Party v. California, 19__

Summary

Briefly summarize the request of the petitioner, in this case the Aryan Party.

Facts

List and number the facts of the case as they have been reported.

Opinion

1. Discuss the implications of the facts in light of the First Amendment. You may introduce this section with the words:

   "The petitioner has claimed that its rights were . . ."

2. Add your comments, using any or all of the three cases you have read as precedents to support your opinion. You may discuss the pros and cons of the argument, using such phrases as "On the one hand . . .; On the other hand. . . ."

3. Conclude by restating the reasons for your opinion. You may begin this part with "I believe that the petitioner's First Amendment rights have/have not been disregarded for these reasons . . ."

THE SECOND DRAFT

Learning about Writing II

EMOTIONALLY CHARGED LANGUAGE

Presenting the facts of a case impartially is important. The description must be both accurate and neutral in tone.

Exercise 1. Recognizing Emotionally Charged Language

A. Words have the power not only to describe events but to affect how we feel about them. Read these sentences out loud.

- Members of the crowd stated that they saw the police raise their clubs before the speaker addressed the crowd.
- The police attacked the demonstrators with clubs flying.

B. Think about the tone of voice you used when you said each one.

1. Which sentence sounds more factual? Which words and phrases help give it this neutral tone?

2. Which sentence did you read more dramatically? Which words help give it this emotional tone?

3. Does the second sentence make you sympathize with the police or with the demonstrators?

4. What impression do verbs like *attacked* and adjectives like *flying* create? How can they influence the way a reader thinks about an event?

Exercise 2. *Identifying Emotionally Charged Words and Phrases*

Read the following statements and identify the emotionally charged words and phrases.

1. The angry mob of hate-filled hecklers forced their way to the speaker's stand.

2. The crazed leader and his rabid followers screamed their terrifying slogans at the crowd.

3. Police officers upheld the law by quietly and efficiently removing the loudest group of protesters.

4. The three young mothers were torn from the group of demonstrators by cops impatient to get the job done.

5. The loud and raucous music incited the listeners to further expressions of violence.

6. The crowd showed its appreciation of the band by dancing with renewed energy and excitement.

Exercise 3. *Finding Additional Examples of Charged Language*

Editorials in newspapers and magazines often use emotionally charged language to influence a reader's opinion. News stories, on the other hand, are supposed to use only factual language. The same event is often described and discussed in both the news section and the editorial section of a paper.

Find examples of both kinds of writing and bring them in for class discussion. Compare the pieces, identifying specific words and phrases that add emotional overtones.

Exercise 4. *Changing Emotionally Charged Language*

Look at Exercise 2 above. Rewrite the first three sentences as a paragraph. Describe the events using neutral, impartial language. Compare your version with a classmate's.

Exercise 5. *Reviewing Your Opinion*

Review the opinion you wrote in the *Aryan Party v. California* case. Did you use a neutral tone to present the facts? Did you avoid using emotionally charged language?

Writing the Second Draft

Read the first draft again. To help you decide what changes to make, ask yourself the following questions or work with a partner to answer these questions about each other's drafts:

- Is the summary clear and complete?
- Are all the important facts in the case listed in neutral language?
- Is your opinion stated clearly, avoiding emotionally charged language?
- Is your opinion supported with precedents?
- Is the argument arranged in a specific order?

Make whatever changes you need in order to improve your essay. You may decide to add, take out, combine, or move some details.

Writing the Final Copy

When you are finished revising, edit your essay for errors in spelling, grammar, and punctuation. If you have not already given your essay a title, add one now. Copy your revised draft neatly on clean paper before you hand it in to your instructor.

One Final Test

When all the papers are in final form your instructor may decide to submit the class work to the best test of all. How convincing are the arguments? One way to determine their effectiveness is to hold a mock trial before a student jury with teams representing each side.

UNIT EIGHT
WRITING A TERM PAPER

PART ONE: DEVELOPING A THESIS

Technology

This is the first of three units in which you will be reading and writing about technology and its relationship to society. Your work in Units Eight, Nine, and Ten will be organized differently than it was in Units One through Seven. In these three units you will be preparing to write a longer paper than you have done so far.

- In Unit Eight, you will read two selections and do some prewriting activities in order to become familiar with the underlying concepts in the three units.

- In Unit Nine, you will read three additional selections and gather information for your paper. At the end of that unit, you will write your first draft.

- In Unit Ten, you will complete some revision activities and write the second draft of your paper.

In this unit you are going to read two selections about the impact of technological change on workers and on the workplace. Both George Woodcock, writing in 1944, and Colin Norman, writing in 1981, express concern that people's lives are often changed for the worse by the very inventions that are meant to improve their lives.

GETTING READY TO WRITE

Before you read the selections in this unit, discuss in small groups some basic concepts and terms.

1. *Natural* is related to the word *nature*, and *mechanical* is related to the word *machine*.

   a. What ideas and qualities do you associate with *nature*? What ideas and qualities do you associate with *machine*?

b. Does *natural* mean "not mechanical"? Does *mechanical* mean "not natural"? Are these two concepts opposites?

c. How would you define *natural*? How would you define *mechanical*? Write one or two sentences to define each word. You might begin like this:

Natural is a word that describes . . .

Natural refers to . . .

Mechanical is a word that describes . . .

Mechanical refers to . . .

2. What does the word *technology* mean to you? Write one or two sentences to define *technology*. You might begin this way:

Technology refers to . . .

Technology is a term for . . .

3. What does the word *monitor* mean in the sentence below? What does the word *control* mean?

Employers are better able to control the rate of production because computers monitor the workers' output.

a. What negative ideas are connected with the word *control*?

b. Does *monitor* make you think of anything negative? If so, what? Is it a more or less negative term than *control*?

4. What does the word *tyranny* mean to you? What do *tyrants* do? Is *tyranny* always a negative word?

5. A figure of speech is a way of using language that is usually based on comparison. Here are three common figures of speech used in the selection by George Woodcock:

Time is money.

as regular as clockwork

kill time

a. In what way is time like money? What happens when you "spend" time doing something?

b. What makes the gears inside a clock so regular, or predictable? In what ways can people be as regular as the mechanism that makes a clock work?

c. What do people do when they "kill" time? What is time being compared to?

I. Time Is Money

"The Tyranny of the Clock" is an essay written by George Woodcock in 1944. According to Woodcock, the clock was the central invention of the industrial age because it was the first completely automatic device to have an important function in society. This essay describes life on the factory floor and the impact of the clock on work and workers.

Before you read the selection, discuss these questions with your classmates.

1. Do you use a clock regularly? What do you use it for? Do you ever feel that the clock controls your life? Does the clock ever interfere with your personal sense of what "on time" and "late" mean?

2. Have you ever worked in a factory? What kind of work did you do? What were the working conditions?

3. How is the clock used to regularize and regiment life in factories and other places of work? Might these uses of the clock ever conflict with a particular culture's definition of "on time" or "late"?

4. Is it necessary to use clocks to keep track of how many hours people work? How would factories and other large organizations operate without clocks?

THE TYRANNY OF THE CLOCK

(1)   In no characteristic is existing society in the West so sharply distinguished from the earlier societies, whether of Europe or the East, than in its conception of time. To the ancient Chinese or Greek, to the Arab herdsman or Mexican people of today, time is represented in the cyclical processes of nature, the alternation of day and night, the passage from season to season. The nomads and farmers measured and still measure their day from sunrise to sunset, and their year in terms of the seedtime and harvest, of the falling leaf and the thawing ice. The farmer worked according to the elements; the craftsman for so long as he felt it necessary to perfect his product. . . .

(2)   Modern Western man, however, lives in a world which runs according to the mechanical and mathematical symbols of clock time. The clock dictates his movement and inhibits his actions. The clock turns time from a process of nature into a commodity that can be measured and bought and sold like soup or sultanas. . . .

(3)   The clock, as Lewis Mumford* points out, represents the key machine of the machine age, both for its influence on technics and for its influence on the habits of men. Technically, the clock was the first really automatic machine that attained any importance in the lives of men. Prior to its invention, the common machines were of such a nature that their operation depended on some external and unreliable force such as human or animal muscle, water or wind. . . . the clock was the first automatic machine that attained a public importance and social function. . . .

*Lewis Mumford (1895–1990) was an influential American sociologist, writer, and critic. His books include *The City in History* and *The Condition of Man.*

"The Tyranny of the Clock" by George Woodcock. Used by permission of the author.

(4)   Socially, the clock had a more radical influence than any other machine in that it was the means by which the regularization and regimentation of life necessary for an exploiting system of industry could best be attained. The new capitalists, in particular, became rapidly time conscious. Time, here symbolizing the work of the laborer, was regarded by them as if it were the chief raw material of industry. "Time is money" became the key slogan of the capitalist ideology, and the timekeeper was the most significant of the new types of officials introduced with capitalism. In the early factories, the employers went so far as to manipulate their clocks or sound their factory whistles at the wrong time in order to defraud the workers of a little of this valuable new commodity. Later such practices became less frequent, but the influence of the clock imposed a regularity on the lives of the majority of men which had previously been known only in the monastery. Men actually became like clocks, acting with a repetitive regularity which had no resemblance to the rhythmic life of a natural being. They became, as the Victorian phrase put it, "as regular as clockwork." . . .

(5)   The introduction of mass produced watches and clocks in the 1850s spread time-consciousness among those who had previously merely reacted to the stimulus of the factory whistle. In the church and the school, in the office and the workshop, punctuality was held up as the greatest of virtues.

(6)   Out of this slavish dependence on mechanical time which spread insidiously into every class in the 19th century there grew up the demoralizing regimentation of life which characterizes factory work today. The man who fails to conform faces social ridicule and economic ruin. If he is late at the factory, the worker will lose his job. Hurried meals, the regular morning and evening scramble for trains and buses, the strain of having to work to time schedules all contribute by digestive and nervous disturbances to ruin health and shorten life. Nor does the financial imposition of regularity tend, in the long run, to greater efficiency. Indeed, the quality of the product is usually much poorer because the employer, regarding time as a commodity which he has yet to pay for, forces the operative to maintain such a speed that his work must necessarily be skimped. Quantity rather than quality becomes the criterion and the enjoyment is taken out of the work itself. In turn, the worker becomes the "clock watcher" concerned only with when he will be able to escape to the scanty and monotonous leisure of industrial society, in which he "kills time" by cramming in as much time-scheduled and mechanized enjoyment of the cinema, radio, and newspaper as his wage and his tiredness will allow. . . .

(7)   The problem of the clock is, in general, similar to that of the machine. Mechanical time is valuable as a means of coordination of activities in a highly developed society, just as the machine is valuable as a means of reducing unnecessary labor to a minimum. Both are valuable for the contribution they make to the smooth running of society and should be used insofar as they assist men to cooperate efficiently and to eliminate monotonous toil and social confusion. But neither should be allowed to dominate men's lives as they do today. Now the movement of the clock sets the tempo of men's lives—they become the servant of the concept of time which they themselves have made. . . . In a sane and free society . . . mechanical time would be relegated to its true function of a means of reference and coordination and men would return again to a balanced view of life no longer dominated by time regulation and the worship of the clock. . . .

THINK AND DISCUSS

Think about the following questions. Then discuss them with your classmates.

1. According to Woodcock, how does the way a clock measures time differ from the way time is measured in societies without clocks? What examples have you observed of these differences in measuring time? (Think about what you read and observed in Unit Two.) What additional changes has the digital clock made in the way we measure time?

2. What pressures does Woodcock say the clock puts on workers? What other examples would you add from your own experience?

3. Woodcock maintains that the clock is used to tyrannize and exploit workers. Do you agree with him? Why or why not?

4. What, according to Woodcock, are the benefits of measuring time by a clock? What other examples would you add from your own experience?

WRITING WARM-UP

In a few sentences, state in your own words the main idea of "The Tyranny of the Clock."

_____

_____

_____

_____

II. The Cost of Technology

This selection contains excerpts from *The God That Limps*, a book that was published in 1981. The author, Colin Norman, is a science writer and an editor of *Science* magazine. The title refers to Hephaestus (the Greek name) or Vulcan (the Roman name), the mythological god of fire and metal-working, who, because of a broken leg, walked with a limp. Norman uses Hephaestus as a symbol of technology.

Before you read the selection, discuss these questions with your classmates.

1. What kinds of jobs have you had? Have you worked with your hands? Have you worked with computers and other electronic equipment?

2. How were you supervised on the jobs you have had? Did someone keep track of how many hours you worked or of how much you produced?

3. Were the jobs you have had satisfying? If you used computers and other electronic devices, in what way did they make your job more satisfying or less satisfying?

4. Do you think technology will make life better or worse in the future?

THE GOD THAT LIMPS

(1)   Studies of the impact of technology on jobs have largely been concerned with aggregate gains and losses; few have looked deeply into impacts on the types of jobs affected and on changes in the quality of worklife. Yet these impacts are likely to be just as important as changes in the total number of jobs. A study conducted for the West German government shows just how sweeping the changes are likely to be in the coming years. The spread of microelectronics could lead to the loss of close to two million jobs in that country in the eighties, the study predicted, but if economic growth remains reasonably strong, a similar number of jobs will be created in occupations associated with computers. The net job impact will not be very great, but the jobs created would require very different skills from those that are lost.

(2)   Technological change has always altered the mix of skills needed in the workforce, but the transition to the computer and information society is expected to involve an unprecedented range of jobs and skills. Already, there are signs of a mismatch in the skill levels available in the workforce and those required by the new technologies, with shortages of computer programmers, people trained in the maintenance of electronic equipment, and similar workers, in the midst of near-record unemployment. Clearly there will be an immense need for retraining in the years ahead. . . .

(3)   [In the past] the development of mass production and the evolution of the assembly line involved the use of technology to organize and rationalize* workers in order to increase efficiency and reduce production costs. One element in this rationalization process is increased control over people on the factory floor as they become consigned to more and more routine tasks that involve little initiative or independent action. The guiding light behind early efforts to organize labor forces in a way that made them unthinking links in a larger process was Frederick Winslow Taylor, an American engineer who coined the term "scientific management." Taylor's ideas, as David Dickson† has pointed out, involved breaking down each task into

*Rationalize: to restructure a job in order to reduce the number of steps or tasks required

†David Dickson (1946–   ) is a British science journalist who has worked for the magazines *Nature*, *Science*, and *New Scientist*.

its component parts and then rearranging these tasks in the most "efficient" manner. His thinking, Dickson writes, "launched a fashion for 'industrial' engineering, particularly in the United Kingdom and the U.S., between 1910 and 1930, resulting in techniques that have since become an essential part of industrial processes almost everywhere. In particular, what we now know as 'automation' is conceptually a logical extension of Taylor's scientific management." . . .

(4)　The spreading of microprocessors and computerized machinery threatens to carry this process even further in some applications, increasing the supervision of workers and further reducing their scope for independent thought and action. In some automobile plants, for example, computers not only control machines, but in many cases, they are also used to control the speed of the production lines and to monitor the output of workers. . . .

(5)　As computerized machinery becomes more and more common in offices, it is likely to lead to changes in the patterns of clerical work, with jobs broken down into parts and work routed in a way that results in maximum efficiency. It will be possible, moreover, for managers to monitor more closely the output of workers—indeed, an advertisement in the United States for a business computer makes much of the fact that a sales manager can call up an instant analysis showing which members of his sales force are performing above or below average.

(6)　There is no immutable reason why technological change should occur in a way that degrades the quality of worklife. But as long as the decisions about the development and introduction of new technology are left solely in the hands of managers, with little or no input from workers, new technologies are likely to increase the hierarchical control of factories and offices. Greater industrial democracy and sharing of decision making are required to ensure that new technologies are not introduced in a way that degrades jobs and de-skills workers.

THINK AND DISCUSS

Think about the following questions. Then discuss them with your classmates.

1. According to Colin Norman, what technological change had the greatest impact on worklife in the 1980s? What impact has this technological change had on your life?

2. What choices do workers have when the nature of their jobs changes because new technologies have been introduced? If you owned a large factory, what would you want to do with workers who were not trained to handle new technologies? If you were a worker, what would you want?

3. According to Colin Norman, what is "scientific management"? Why do you think it became common with the rise of industrialization?

4. How are computers used to monitor and control workers? What effect do you think this kind of monitoring and control has on workers? (Think about what you read and discussed in Unit Six.)

5. How do you think work has changed for most people in the last ten years? What kinds of changes do you think will occur in the next ten years?

6. Why do you think Colin Norman uses Hephaestus as a symbol of technology? That is, why did he title his book *The God That Limps*?

WRITING WARM-UP

In a few sentences, state in your own words the main idea of this selection from *The God That Limps*.

_____

_____

_____

_____

PREWRITING
Preparing to Write a Term Paper

In the preceding units, you have become familiar with most of the steps in writing an essay. Now you are ready to put them all together, along with a few additional steps, in order to produce a longer, more complicated piece of writing. Your assignment will be to write a paper in which you do three things:

1. Examine issues related to the question: How have technological advances affected workers and their environment?

2. State which issue you think is the most important.

3. Explain why you think this issue is important.

A paper like this is sometimes called a *term paper* because it draws together the reading and thinking you have been doing over a school term. Another way to describe a paper like this is to call it a *position paper* because in it you take a position, or express an opinion, on a complex issue.

Discuss the following questions.

1. Test questions frequently ask you to take a position and support it. What other kinds of writing are you familiar with that are examples of a position paper?

2. What is the question you will be taking a position on in this paper?

Exercise 1: *Discovering What You Have Learned*

Work in small groups. Read the list of tasks below. Then discuss the activities or writing assignments you have done so far that might help you with these tasks:

- gathering ideas and information to use in your writing
- summarizing and paraphrasing someone else's point of view
- expressing your own point of view
- supporting your point of view with facts and examples
- supporting your point of view with quotations
- comparing and contrasting two or more examples
- making a generalization about a group of examples

DEVELOPING A PRELIMINARY THESIS

The activities below will help you find information in the reading selections that you will need when you write your paper. They will also help you develop a preliminary, or working, thesis.

Exercise 2: *Identifying Problems*

Answer each question by making notes. Keep your notes. You will use them when you write.

1. In paragraph 2, George Woodcock identifies one problem caused by the clock: the clock turns time into something that can be bought and sold. According to this selection, what other problems were created by the invention of the clock? Look especially at what Woodcock says about the following:

   clocks in factories (paragraph 4)

   regimentation of life (paragraphs 4, 5, and 6)

   quality of products (paragraph 6)

2. In paragraphs 1 and 2, Colin Norman identifies one of the results of technological change: the new jobs created by new technologies demand very different skills than the workers needed for their old jobs. According to Norman, what problems are introduced when technology is used to increase efficiency? (see paragraphs 3, 4, and 5)

Exercise 3: *Brainstorming Additional Examples*

The answers you wrote in Exercise 2 gave you some specific examples of problems created by technological change in the workplace. Brainstorm with your classmates. Make a list of the problems created by technology that you have encountered yourself.

If you have ever worked in a factory, think about how your production was measured. You can also include problems you have read about in books, magazines, or newspapers. Remember that for this paper, you are limited to the effect of technology on workers and the workplace.

Drawing examples from reading and from personal experience is a first step in writing a term paper. In order for the examples to be useful, however, they need to be grouped in some way. The easiest way to create groups is to look for examples that form part of the same general idea.

Exercise 4: Grouping Examples

Look through all the examples you listed in Exercises 2 and 3. Which ones belong in the same group? Rewrite your lists, grouping together all the examples that belong together. You should have at least three groups or categories.

Here is a model. On the left is part of the long list of examples a student might have written in Exercises 2 and 3. On the right are the examples this student has grouped together because they are all in the category of things that make workers dissatisfied with their jobs.

Examples of Problems

the workplace looks different

people work in isolation

some people may lose their jobs

the work is repetitive

new skills are needed

workers can't make decisions

communication is faster

. . .

Group 1

people work in isolation

the work is repetitive

workers can't make decisions

Exercise 5: Developing Generalizations

Putting your examples into groups helps you make generalizations that describe what the examples have in common. For example, Group 1 in the preceding exercise included:

people work in isolation

the work is repetitive

workers can't make decisions

They all show why workers are dissatisfied with their jobs. Here are two generalizations that can be made to describe this group:

Work is unsatisfying

Quality of worklife is poor

Next to each group of examples you wrote in Exercise 4 write a generalization. If you think of more than one generalization for any group, write them all.

Exercise 6: Developing a Preliminary Thesis

Reread your generalizations and the examples grouped under them. Make a preliminary decision—based on the reading, thinking, and discussing you have done so far—about which problem you think is the most important. Then use the generalization and examples to complete the following statement:

Technology has had a profound impact on the workplace. I think the most important problem is _____ because _____.
                               (generalization)   (examples)

Exercise 7: Expanding the Preliminary Thesis

Write the first draft of a paragraph to explain and expand your preliminary thesis. Here are some of the things you might do in this paragraph:

- provide some background information about the problem you have chosen
- add some details to the examples you have given
- indicate which example you think is the most important and why

When you have finished your draft, exchange papers with a classmate. Discuss these questions:

- Is the thesis clear?
- Do the examples support the thesis?

Make whatever changes are needed in your thesis and examples. Keep this draft. When you have finished the reading in Unit Nine, you may want to revise this paragraph and use it in your final paper.

As you begin to read and take notes on the selections in Unit Nine, use your preliminary thesis to guide you. Remember that this thesis is just a starting point. The additional information in Unit Nine will help you decide a number of things:

- whether you have identified the problem correctly
- whether this problem is in fact the most important one
- whether something is equally important or more important

UNIT NINE
WRITING A TERM PAPER

PART TWO: GATHERING AND ORGANIZING INFORMATION

Technology

In Unit Eight, you became familiar with some of the issues related to the impact of technology on the workplace and developed an initial thesis for a term paper. Your writing assignment in this unit will be to write the first draft of a term paper in which you do the following things:

♦ examine the way technological advances have affected workers and their environment and identify the key issues

♦ state which issue you think is the most important

♦ explain why you think this issue is important

The three articles you will read in this unit provide additional information needed to support the position you take in your paper. You may also use any other books or articles you have read on this subject.

GETTING READY TO WRITE

Study the chart on page 135. It shows the steps you need to take in order to develop a thesis and write a clear draft. Then discuss the following questions with your classmates.

1. Which steps involve acquiring background information to write your paper?

2. Which steps involve writing and refining your thesis?

3. What should you do if you are not ready to develop a preliminary thesis?

4. What should you do if you are having trouble supporting your thesis?

5. What should you do after you have writen your final thesis statement?

6. Which steps did you do in Unit Eight?

7. After looking at the chart, do you feel prepared to begin the steps you will be doing in Unit Nine? If not, what should you do?

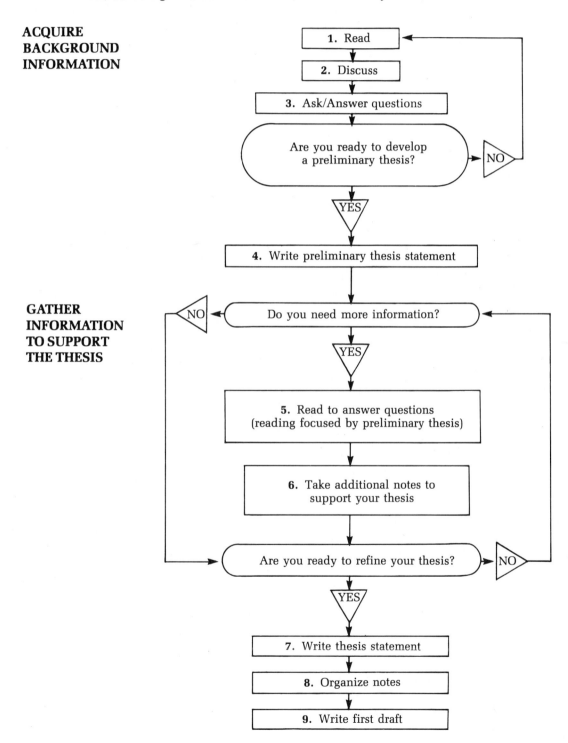

ACQUIRE
BACKGROUND
INFORMATION

1. Read

2. Discuss

3. Ask/Answer questions

Are you ready to develop a preliminary thesis?

NO

YES

4. Write preliminary thesis statement

GATHER
INFORMATION
TO SUPPORT
THE THESIS

NO ← Do you need more information?

YES

5. Read to answer questions
(reading focused by preliminary thesis)

6. Take additional notes to support your thesis

Are you ready to refine your thesis?

NO

YES

7. Write thesis statement

8. Organize notes

9. Write first draft

THE FIRST DRAFT

Learning about Writing I

An issue is something that is in dispute—something with two or more sides. An issue is not itself a problem, but it often sums up or groups together a number of problems. In order to analyze issues, you need to be able to identify problems and their causes. Your first job in writing this paper, then, is to be sure that you recognize causes and effects.

IDENTIFYING AND ANALYZING ISSUES: TECHNOLOGY AND TRAINING

Training is an issue related to technological change in the workplace. This issue includes the problem of untrained workers being unable to handle new technology. Another way to describe this problem is to label its parts in this way:

Causes:	introduction of new technology
	lack of training
Effect:	workers unable to handle job

Before you read the selection, "The Growth of the Global Office" by Steve Lohr, discuss the problem of technology and training with your classmates. What other problems might the issue of training include?

THE GROWTH OF THE GLOBAL OFFICE

(1)   For the New York Life Insurance Company, the office of the future is in this rural Irish market village [Castleisland], where high technology has usually meant a new tractor.

(2)   New York Life came here largely because it was having trouble finding enough skilled workers to process insurance claims in the United States. Ireland, on the other hand, has a large pool of well-educated young people who need jobs and are willing to work for wages lower than those that must be paid in the United States. So since July, New York Life has been processing claims from Castleisland, using a computer link to its processing center in New Jersey.

Forefront of Movement

(3)   The step puts New York Life in the forefront of the development of the "global office," the movement of office jobs abroad to take advantage of lower pay scales and other costs. The movement could have a sweeping effect on how and where white-collar work is done in the future.

(4)   Behind the development are recent improvements in telecommunications and computer technology that permit many office jobs to be performed thousands of miles from where the work is needed.

(5)   With the new technology, service industries could follow the route taken for more than a decade by manufacturing industries, which have large parts of their products made more cheaply abroad.

(6)   Corporate executives and business experts believe that the fast-growing services sector of the economy is ripe for such globalization. They say that the handful of companies that have already set up offices abroad, like New York Life, will be followed by many others.

(7)   "This is a phenomenon that has just begun," said D. Quinn Mills, a Harvard Business School professor. "You'll see a lot more of it. And there are very few limits to how far it can go."

(8)   Ireland has made it national policy to attract American companies seeking foreign locations for office work. In addition to the New York Life operation, which combines data entry with analysis, the Industrial Development Authority of Ireland has focused on luring companies to set up computer software operations. Last year, for example, the Travelers Corporation, a Hartford-based insurer, opened an office in Castleroy to write software for its own use. McGraw-Hill, Inc., the New York-based publishing house, last July began processing subscription renewal and marketing information for several of its magazines in Galway. Others, like Boeing and Bechtel, have also set up software development offices for their own use.

(9)   To be sure, computer and software companies, including I.B.M., Microsoft, and Lotus, had previously established offices in Ireland. But these were primarily to develop a production base for international sales and were not in the global-office mold.

High Employee Turnover

(10)   But the forces pushing corporations to send white-collar work abroad go well beyond the wage benefits, as shown by the New York Life case. With unemployment low, especially in the New York region, the company found that recruiting workers for low-level jobs like claims processing became more and more difficult. Moreover, employee turnover in claims offices in the industry is high, as much as 30 percent a year. And changing demographic trends will aggravate the problem. In the decade ending in 1995, the number of 18- to 24-year-olds in the American work force will decline by 17.5 percent.

(11)   "The demographics make this a nationwide challenge," said John Foy, a vice president of New York Life. "American companies will find it much more difficult to find skilled workers at home for the rest of this century."

(12)   The development of the global office has been an evolutionary process. For years, many companies have moved some "back office" clerical, accounting, and data processing operations out of urban heaquarters sites, where office and housing costs are high. And American executives have begun using portable computers, telefax machines, and the like to work from home or while traveling so they can stay in touch, electronically, with their offices.

(13)　The additional technological advances of satellite communications and trans-oceanic fiber optic cables now make it reasonable for corporations to view each of their many service functions separately and ask: Where in the world can a certain task be done most efficiently and at the lowest cost?

'Extensions of the U.S.'

(14)　"More and more companies are looking at foreign countries as extensions of the U.S.," said Paul Coombes, a principal of McKinsey & Company, the consulting firm. "Technology has enabled corporate management to make sourcing and location decisions internationally in ways that they could not before."

(15)　To date, there has been no social or political resistance to the globalization of white collar work, perhaps because the trend is still in its infancy. But analysts say that if it appears that companies are reducing American employment in favor of lower wage rates overseas, then public and political resistance is likely.

(16)　The office tasks taken abroad range from the rudimentary entering of information into a computer system to the development of software by university-trained computer scientists. The more basic functions went overseas first. For example, Saztec International, Inc., an information conversion concern that has computerized the cataloguing system of the New York Public Library and the Getty Museum, set up an operation in the Philippines in 1979. Today, Saztec employs 300 people in Manila.

(17)　"Data entry and coding can be done anywhere in the world today," said Thomas I. Reed, Saztec's chairman.

(18)　Another early entrant, American Airlines, decided four years ago that it could save money by sending its ticket stubs to the Caribbean, where keyboard operators type the flight information into a computer, instead of having higher-paid workers do that at American's data processing center in Tulsa, Oklahoma.

(19)　American's data-entry operation, Caribbean Data Services, is a subsidiary of the airline's parent company, the AMR Corporation. Employing 1,050 workers in Barbados and the Dominican Republic, Caribbean Data Services is now an independent profit maker for AMR, handling data entry for outside customers as well as for the airline.

(20)　The global offices in Ireland are still in an experimental stage. But the obstacles to growth have more to do with traditional corporate views than with the difficulties of adjusting to new technology, executives say.

(21)　Travelers opened its software development office in July 1987. It now has a staff of 27, nearly all of them young Irish computer scientists. The office has performed well, said Peter C. Noonan, managing director of Travelers of Ireland, Ltd., but he has noticed that attitudes toward sending software chores to Ireland vary considerably from department to department in Hartford.

(22)　"You've got to earn the credibility within the company," Mr. Noonan said. "Here, you're not just a little removed from headquarters. You're in Ireland.

(23)　"You can do this technologically, but the question is attitudes. What it takes are people and companies willing to try it."

(24)　Management experts, for example, note that top executives often find it difficult to relinquish the "galley slave" mentality—the view that unless workers are under the physical eye of the boss, efficiency suffers.

Breaking Down the Prejudices

(25)　Still, traditional prejudices often melt when executives are confronted with the economic advantages of the global office. One example: computer science graduates in Ireland earn an average salary of $14,000, according to the Irish development authority. Their counterparts on the East or West Coasts of the United States earn twice as much.

(26)　Moreover, the unemployment rate in Ireland is 19 percent, more than three times the level in America.

(27)　Mr. Foy of New York Life, an Irishman who emigrated to the United States 20 years ago, examined the economics of setting up in Ireland. He estimated that telecommunications charges would be three times as high in Ireland and the bill for shipping the insurance claim forms to Ireland by air would be $50,000 a year. Still, he put the cost of the Castleisland operation at 20 percent below a similar one in the United States.

(28)　"As I looked at it closely, it seemed that we would be foolish not to try going to Ireland," Mr. Foy said.

(29)　When New York Life placed an advertisement in an Irish paper last May to fill 25 jobs, it received 600 applications. The company now employs 52 people in Castleisland, mostly Irish women in their early 20's. They work as claims processors.

(30)　When the medical claims arrive in Castleisland, workers enter the information into personal computers linked by a trans-Atlantic line to the company's data processing center in Clinton, N.J. Aided by the company's computer programs, the workers determine claims and amounts—decisions that are transmitted instantly to the United States.

(31)　Cathy O'Grady, a 23-year-old native of Castleisland, finds the work more stimulating than her two previous jobs, as a part-time tour guide at an Irish heritage museum and teaching English in Spain. "Faraway hills are green," Ms. O'Grady said, "but I missed home. I like it here and now I have a job as well."

Exercise 1: Identifying Causes and Effects

Write the answers to the following questions about "The Growth of the Global Office." Paraphrase or summarize the information in the text rather than use the author's exact words. Keep your answers. They can be used as notes on the reading when you begin to write.

1. According to paragraph 2, what problem did New York Life Insurance Company face initially?

2. What was New York Life's solution to this problem? What role did technology play in the solution?

3. According to the article, what are the reasons that New York Life Insurance and other companies like it have chosen this solution? In what paragraphs do you find these reasons given?

4. What additional problem might this solution create? In what paragraph is this problem identified?

IDENTIFYING AND ANALYZING ISSUES: TECHNOLOGY AND COST REDUCTION

When you examine the issues related to technological change, you need to be able to identify the advantages and disadvantages of various technological advances. Sometimes, the advantages and disadvantages are stated. Other times, they are only implied, or suggested by the facts and examples that are given.

Before you read the next selection, "Calling Collect? A Computer Is at Your Service," by Calvin Sims, discuss the following questions with your classmates:

1. What is a collect call? What is a third-party call?

2. Have you ever made a telephone call that was answered by a computer? What are the advantages and disadvantages of such a system?

3. Have you encountered computers on other occasions when you expected a human being? Which do you prefer?

CALLING COLLECT? A COMPUTER IS AT YOUR SERVICE

(1)   Human telephone operators are rapidly disappearing, hastened on their way by new equipment that can both recognize and mimic the human voice.

(2)   In the latest twist, several regional and local telephone companies around the nation are beginning to offer customers an electronic operator system that allows them to make, through a computer, collect calls and calls billed to a third party.

(3)   In May, Michigan Bell became the first company to offer such a service. The BellSouth Corporation, which serves the Southeast, will introduce the system later this year, and the Nynex Corporation plans to offer a computerized operator system in New York and New England late next year.

(4)   The telephone companies contend that the systems will greatly reduce the need for human operators and the cost of completing calls at a time when the number of collect and third-party calls is increasing. But union leaders say the new technology will provide an excuse for layoffs, and others question the quality of service provided by electronic operators.

(5)   The savings will be only for the companies; calling rates are not expected to fall.

(6)   "This was bound to happen sooner or later because it's just too expensive for phone companies to keep completing these types of calls with human operators," said John Reddy, a business professor at the Wilkes-Barre campus of Pennsylvania State University.

(7)   Mr. Reddy, who spent 25 years as a strategic planner in operator services with the old Bell system, predicted that electronic operators would "eventually replace about half of the estimated 70,000 operators employed by local and long-distance phone companies across the nation."

(8)   For now, though, it is a local phenomenon. The nation's three leading long-distance companies—AT&T, MCI, and US Sprint—say they have no immediate plans to use the technology because consumers place a high value on human operators. Because of the stiff competition in the long-distance industry, the carriers are afraid to offend customers by introducing electronic operators. The regional companies have a monopoly on local service and face no such competition.

(9)   Using voice synthesis and voice recognition technology, the electronic operator can make collect and third-party calls. It relies on the caller's response from a push-button keypad, similar to the way the current network processes calls made with a credit card.

How a Collect Call Is Made

(10)   To make a collect call, for example, a caller dials 0, the area code, and the seven-digit number. The caller then punches 1 on the keypad to alert the electronic operator that a collect call is desired. The computer then asks the caller to state whom the call is from, records the caller's response, and waits for the called party to answer.

(11)   The computer informs the called party that there is a collect call, plays back the name of the caller, and instructs the party to answer yes or no to accept or reject the call.

(12)   The automated system recognizes the caller's response and processes the call accordingly. The system, made by Northern Telecom, Inc., compares the caller's response with thousands of yes and no responses on a digital template.

(13)   Michigan Bell said it spent about $2 million to install the system, while other companies declined to give any figures.

(14)   A caller can reach a live operator at any point by dialing a designated number on the keypad. Live operators are needed in emergency situations, when callers are connected to a wrong number or when the call does not go through.

No Staff Cutbacks Planned

(15)   Telephone company executives say that they have no plans to reduce the number of operators on staff and that the electronic service is part of an effort to reduce the rising cost of providing live operators. Demand for operator-assisted calls is increasing dramatically, as are labor and benefit costs for live operators.

(16)   The executives say they expect the electronic service to cut overhead costs by more than half, eliminating the need to hire additional operators to handle the increasing number of collect and third-party calls.

(17)   Despite the expected savings for the phone companies, consumers should not expect to pay less for such calls. The companies say they plan to use any savings that result from the technology to keep the cost of operator-assisted calls from rising.

(18)   "We are introducing this new service to keep our costs for operator services under control," said Phil Jones, a spokesman for Michigan Bell. "It will allow us to continue processing these calls at no extra increase to consumers."

(19)   Whether a human or electronic operator handles the call, the surcharges for collect and third-party calls will remain the same. New York Telephone assesses a surcharge of $1.20 to $1.48 for collect and credit-card calls that require a live operator. The surcharge for third-party calls, in which a live operator charges the call to another phone number, is $1.23. By comparison, a credit-card call that is processed electronically has a surcharge of 30 cents.

(20)   The Communications Workers of America, the giant telephone employees union, said that while it does not oppose the advent of new technology, it believes that local telephone companies will use the electronic operator system specifically to eliminate jobs and achieve cost savings that they will not share with consumers.

(21)   "Consumers are being asked to do most of the work to make such calls and yet they are reaping none of the benefits," said Dina Beaumont, executive assistant for the union.

(22)   "It's like offering fast-food telephone service at gourmet prices, and they are taking an enormous risk if they think consumers will put up with the diminution of service," said Ms. Beaumont, who was an operator for 30 years with Pacific Telesis, which provides local service to the West Coast.

(23)   Thomas LLoyd, Nynex's director of operator services, said the new technology would not only keep the cost of third-party and collect calls from rising but also allow them to make these calls twice as fast as they can with human operators. "Consumers always have the option of switching to a live operator if they are feeling lazy or need special assistance," Mr. Lloyd said.

60 Percent Prefer the Computer

(24)   In an early trial of the automated system by Southern Bell in Atlanta, a survey of consumers found that when given a choice between a live operator and an electronic one, 60 percent preferred the automated systems.

(25)   Customers who chose the electronic operator said that they did so because it was a much quicker way of completing the call and that they did not like dealing with human operators. Consumers who chose human operators said they found the automated system disorienting because they expected a human operator to handle the call.

(26)   At the American Telephone and Telegraph Company, Jim Selzer, vice president of operator services, said: "Operators are a value-added service and we use them as differentiators. If we introduced electronic operators for these calls, many of our customers would see it as a slight and would be more inclined to use our competitors."

(27)   Dan Evanoff, US Sprint's vice president of services, said the cost of providing operator services would be "15 times cheaper" with an automated system. "But we are willing to pay a substantially higher cost for what customers describe as higher-quality service," Mr. Evanoff said. "We esteem customer satisfaction so highly that we are not going to flirt with something that has not been proven."

(28)   AT&T, the nation's largest long-distance carrier, charges $1.75 for credit-card calls that involve a live operator but only 80 cents for credit-card calls made using an automated system.

(29)   Collect calls represent about 50 percent of AT&T's operator-assisted calls, with credit-card calls accounting for 25 percent and the remainder going to third-party and person-to-person calls. The regional companies declined to disclose the breakdown of operator-assisted calls.

(30)   Mr. Reddy of Penn State said about 20 percent of all collect calls in the United States originate from prisons, which are the only type of calls that most correctional institutions allow. College students, military personnel, and travelers account for nearly all of the remainder.

Process Began in 1950's

(31)   AT&T has been reducing the size of its operator force since the 1950's, when it introduced direct long-distance dialing, which eliminated the need for operators to make connections. In the early 1970's, AT&T installed an automatic distribution system for operator-assisted calls that significantly reduced the handling time for each call. The advent of computerized directory systems in 1975 meant that operators no longer had to flip through telephone books.

(32)   The 1980's brought verification systems that allow customers to charge calls without operator intervention and audio response units that state phone numbers for directory assistance. Following the 1984 breakup of the Bell system, AT&T started transferring operators to the regional companies to handle long-distance calls within a state.

Exercise 2: Identifying Advantages and Disadvantages

Write the answers to the questions below. Remember to paraphrase or summarize the information in the text. Keep your answers to use as notes for your paper.

1. **a.** What advantages and disadvantages of the electronic operator system are stated in paragraphs 4 and 5?
   b. What additional information about these advantages and disadvantages is given in paragraphs 16 and 17? In paragraphs 21 through 23?
   c. Who benefits from the advantages? Who suffers from the disadvantages?

2. Paragraph 8 explains why the electronic operator system is being tried only by local telephone companies.

   a. According to this paragraph, why don't the long-distance carriers want to use electronic operators?

   b. What disadvantage to the consumer does this imply?

3. Paragraph 19 states what New York Telephone's charges for collect and third-party calls will be, whether they are handled by a human operator or an electronic one. Paragraph 28 states what AT&T's charges are for credit-card calls handled by a human operator and those handled electronically.

   a. What do these figures imply about the advantages to the phone company of New York Telephone's system?

   b. What do they imply about the disadvantage to the consumer?

Exercise 3: *Evaluating Information*

In a paper that identifies and analyzes issues, you sometimes need to form your own judgments about the facts and examples in your resource material. This evaluation can be used to support your analysis of the issues.

Use "The Growth of the Global Office" and "Calling Collect? A Computer Is at Your Service" to answer the following questions. The questions will help you weigh, or evaluate, the information you have been given. Write your answers and save them as notes for your paper.

1. Both of the following reasons might explain New York Life Insurance Company's decision to move its claims processing operations to Castleisland, Ireland.

   • The company was not able to find enough skilled workers in the United States.

   • The company was able to save money by having the work done in Ireland.

   a. Which do you think is the more important reason? Why? If they seem equally important to you, pick the one you can support most easily.

   b. Which paragraphs in "The Growth of the Global Office" support your opinion?

2. Paragraphs 24 and 25 of "Calling Collect? A Computer Is at Your Service" give the results of a survey to determine customer reaction to the electronic operator.

   a. Which response—that of customers who preferred the electronic operator or that of customers who preferred the human operator—is more convincing to you? Why?

   b. Which paragraphs of the article support your opinion?

IDENTIFYING AND ANALYZING ISSUES: TECHNOLOGY AND EMPLOYMENT

The last selection, "Automation of America's Offices, 1985–2000," consists of excerpts from a report published in 1985 by the Congress of the United States. Before you read it, discuss the following questions with your classmates.

1. In what ways can office work be speeded up by technology? In what ways can it be completely automated?

2. What did you learn in "The Growth of the Global Office" about how technology can change office work?

3. Have you ever been a part-time or temporary worker? What are the advantages and disadvantages of this kind of work?

AUTOMATION OF AMERICA'S OFFICES, 1985–2000

How Office Automation Affects Employment

(1)   Office automation can substitute for labor, supplement labor, or reorganize work and thereby make labor more efficient. It can allow highly technical, knowledge-intensive work to be done by relatively untrained and unskilled, lower paid workers. . . . It can change the characteristics and skills associated with occupations and alter their role and relative importance to an industry. It can allow office work to be done away from the office and outside of conventional office hours, even outside of the country.

(2)   The most dramatic potential substitution of technology for labor, in the future, could be the elimination of a large proportion of today's data-entry work (either numeric or text) by:

- interorganizational transfer of data, directly from computer to computer;

- direct input of data by optical scanning technologies, and possibly by speech recognition technology; and

- capture of data at the point of origin, in a variety of ways ranging from bar code readers to consumer use of terminals, e.g., bank automated teller machines (ATMs). . . .

Emerging Occupational Shifts

(3)   Other things being equal, the introduction of labor-saving technology is most likely to cause displacement where the task that is automated has constituted all, or

U.S. Congress, Office of Technology Assessment, "Automation of America's Offices, 1985–2000", OTA-CIT-287 (Springfield, VA: National Technical Information Service, December 1985).

nearly all, of the responsibilities of a given job. In other words, the more narrow and specialized the job, the more likely the job-holder is to be displaced by automation. This applies, at least potentially, to professional specialists as well as to clerical workers. Highly specialized knowledge is potentially most appropriate for incorporation into an expert system (a special software for decision-making) while broad, general knowledge is difficult to incorporate.

(4)   When word processing is introduced, assuming that the workload does not increase, fewer dedicated typists (keyboarders) will be needed. A general secretary who spends only a part of her time typing is not likely to be displaced by a word processor; more likely she will have more time for other responsibilities and may take on new ones. Secretarial positions have been increasing throughout the two decades of office automation, while "typist" jobs are decreasing. . . .

(5)   In the first stage of automation (large computers), the tendency was to make affected jobs more narrowly defined—in other words, to rationalize work. Batch data processors did not learn or do other work. Word processors were set apart in word processing centers. New specialties were created, ranging from computer operators to programmers, and the holders of those jobs typically did nothing else. If data-entry work is completely automated (e.g., by optical scanning technology) those who do only data entry are most likely to be displaced and secretaries are unlikely to be displaced by that development. . . .

(6)   . . . Second phase automation—end-user computing—appears less likely to rationalize tasks or to narrow jobs. Personal computers can be used to integrate tasks and broaden jobs. Moreover, organizations that rationalized work during their early office automation are in some cases using further automation to reverse that process. Many firms have decided that computer and communication technologies are often most effective in reducing costs when control, communication, and decision-making are decentralized and when hierarchic organization and functional specialization of tasks are reduced. They are experimenting with the elimination of both low-skill clerical jobs and routine technical/professional jobs, and with the creation of new multiactivity, skilled clerical positions. In some insurance firms, the result of task reintegration has been a significant reduction in unit labor requirements and an increase in the average skill levels of the remaining clerical, sales, and professional work force. . . .

Part-Time and Temporary Employment

(7)   The proportion of part-time and temporary workers has been increasing since the early 1950s. The number of voluntary part-time workers has remained between 13 and 14 percent since 1970 but the proportion of involuntary part-time workers has continued to increase, indicating that the strongest factor in the growth is not workers' choice of a more flexible lifestyle but employers' response to economic pressures. In some industries and some organizations, slack workloads lead employers to convert workers to part-time in preference to a layoff. Other employers, however, are adopting a policy of keeping a minimum-size work force, which can be temporarily augmented when necessary.

(8)   There are reports that in other industrialized countries automation has greatly increased part-time work; for example in Japan, "introduction of part-time workers and

subcontraction has grown massively." Office automation and creation of a part-time work force are in some situations alternative or competing strategies for cost-cutting but they may also be complementary. Part-time workers (considered by BLS [Bureau of Labor Statistics] as an employee working less than 35 hours a week) are cheaper than a proportionately smaller number of full-time employees because they often are paid lower wages and do not qualify for benefits packages, regular yearly wage increases, or job security agreements based on seniority. . . . The biggest advantage of part-time workers for employers, however, is that of load-leveling; that is, they can be used during parts of the day or week when the workload is heaviest. To the extent that office automation allows the work force to be reduced and workflow made more efficient, it may obviate some interest in working toward a part-time work force.

(9)   But in other situations, office automation encourages the creation of a part-time work force. Where it is used to standardize and de-skill work, many employers have found it profitable to use part-time, low-paid workers. Some have reportedly moved to suburban locations to take advantage of the availability of housewives willing and eager to work part-time at low wages because there is another primary wage-earner, with a full benefits package, in the family. . . . Office automation also makes it feasible to use home-based workers, on a part-time and piece-rate basis. In the long run, office automation may stimulate a stronger trend toward use of part-time or temporary workers by allowing employees to maintain a minimum work force that will need supplementing during hours or seasons of work overload; and by standardizing the basic skills needed by clerical workers and some kinds of professional and technical workers. . . .

(10)   Closely related to part-time work is temporary work, which for employers is another strategy for workload leveling. Many clerical workers are temporaries, but there is a growing trend toward using temporary programmers, systems analysts, computer engineers, and data communications sepcialists. Temporary workers can be called in on short notice when work is briefly or seasonally heavy, and can be dismissed almost instantly and without penalty. From the employer's viewpoint temporaries are part-time workers for whom the organization has no responsibility for long-range job security. The worker who is individually hired on a temporary basis generally suffers the disadvantages of a part-time worker—i.e., not qualifying for benefits and relatively little chance of promotion, and by definition has no job security. . . .

(11)   Part-time and temporary employment and independent contracting are likely to increase as automated offices move toward a lean work force with need for occasional supplementary business services, and as more workers are familiar with the equipment. There are strong benefits in it for workers as well as for employers. Many people prefer and actively seek part-time work. Students, mothers, and retired people often want more time for families, education, or recreation. They choose to trade income for leisure time, and are willing to pay the additional costs in terms of loss of benefits such as health insurance, lack of job security, and diminished likelihood of promotion and advancement. The standard 40 hour workweek has not changed since the 1930s, and part-time work is the way some people create their own shorter work week.

(12)   Many "temporaries" choose this form of employment because they want or need the flexibility it gives them. Some use it as a form of job-hunting, or trying out

potential employers. However, some temporaries are unable to get assignments as regularly as they wish, and find the unpredictability of their income a severe disadvantage, but they have been unable to find permanent employment.

(13)   At a minimum, part-time work is preferable to unemployment. Employers sometimes convert full-time employees to part-time status during a recession, in preference to laying them off and losing a valuable worker.

(14)   If part-time work is beneficial to many employers and is sought by many employees, under what conditions is it a public policy concern? First, if enough full-time jobs are eliminated—i.e., converted to part-time jobs, opportunities will be diminished for those who must have full-time work to make enough money to support themselves and their dependents. Second, in the United States, many social services and income protection mechanisms are provided not directly by taxpayers but through employee benefits packages—e.g., health insurance, life insurance, income during illness or childbirth, pension plans, and to some extent training and higher education. These protections are much more costly, if they are available at all, on an individual basis. If conversion to part-time work means that a sizable proportion of the population no longer has these protections through employment, then the taxpayer is in the long run likely to bear more of the burden of illness, old age, and death for these people, and the average level of health and well-being of the population is likely to decline.

(15)   Society may be willing to bear this risk, if that is the price of allowing people to choose part-time work. If part-time work is not a choice, but the only alternative available to them, and especially if this limitation on choice is the result of employers' decisions, then the public policy issue becomes one of whether this shifting of responsibility for basic protections from employer to employee is acceptable to the society at large. Historically, the choice of full-time or part-time work has been regarded as the individual's prerogative. We must then ask: is this still a free choice, and will it be so in the future? To what extent is *involuntary* part-time work increasing?

USING INFORMATION FROM DIFFERENT SOURCES

Your first draft will draw on information from a number of sources—the two reading selections in Unit Eight, the three selecions in this unit, and any additional books or articles you may have read. In order to support each of the points in your paper effectively, you will often need to give more than one example and use more than one source.

Exercise 4: Selecting Information from Different Sources

Write the answers to the questions below. Remember to paraphrase or summarize the information in the text. Keep your answers as notes for your paper.

Suppose that you have been given the following topic for an essay:

How does technology redefine jobs or change the range of jobs available to workers?

1. Paragraphs 8 and 9 explain two ways that office automation can affect the pattern of employment: by making it possible to reduce the size of the work force and by encouraging the creation of a part-time work force. What details in paragraphs 8 and 9 would you use to answer this question in your essay?

2. What other paragraphs in this selection contain details that would help support your viewpoint?

3. Which paragraphs in selections I and II of this unit contain details that you could use along with the details from selection III?

Exercise 5: *Combining Information from Different Sources*

Read the sentences below. They contain information that could be used to answer the question, "How does technology redefine jobs or change the range of jobs available to workers?" The information is taken from the three reading selections in this unit.

Statements from Reading Selections

1. The electronic operator system may eliminate jobs for human telephone operators.

2. People whose jobs consist of tasks that can be easily automated are most likely to be displaced by technology.

3. Since 1975, telephone operators have been using computerized directories instead of telephone books to look for numbers.

4. Advances in computer technology now make it possible for many office jobs to be done overseas, where costs are lower.

5. The use of bank automated teller machines (ATMs) is one example of the way technology can change people's jobs.

6. Ireland has a large group of educated, skilled workers willing to work for less money than American workers.

7. Since the 1950s, AT&T has been increasing the number of automatic systems and reducing the number of human telephone operators.

8. American Airlines has been sending data-entry work to the Caribbean instead of to its data processing center in Oklahoma.

Now look at the example. Notice how the example combines information from the three reading selections to answer the question about technology and redefining jobs. The first part of the example is a general statement taken from sentence 2 above. The rest consists of examples taken from statements 5 and 1:

> People whose jobs are made up of specialized tasks may have their jobs redefined by automation; for example, bank tellers can be replaced by ATMs, and telephone operators can be replaced by electronic operator systems.

**Now write three sentences, combining information from the
reading selections, to answer the question: How does
technology redefine jobs or change the range of jobs
available to workers? You can use each statement in this
exercise more than once.**

REFINING YOUR THESIS

You have had a chance to read all the background material, to take notes, and
to practice some of the strategies—such as combining sources—that you will
need to write your draft. Now is the time to return to your preliminary thesis
statement and make the final preparations for writing your first draft.

Exercise 6: Identifying Issues

**The first step in refining your thesis is to decide which issue
you plan to write about. Working with your classmates,
follow these steps:**

1. List all the issues you have read about in Units Eight and Nine. You can
   also include issues you are familiar with from your own reading or from
   personal experience.

2. Discuss each issue. Try to answer the question, Why is this issue
   important?

3. Decide which issue you personally think is most important. This is the
   issue you will write about.

When you developed your preliminary thesis in Unit Eight, you probably made
a very general statement. Now that you have more information about the topic,
you can refine your thesis. If your topic is too big and your thesis statement
is too general, it may be difficult to write about it in a convincing and informative way. The following exercises will help you balance general statements
with specific details.

Exercise 7: Exploring Related Ideas

The topic "The Impact of Technology on the Workplace" is a very broad one
that has many related ideas. With your classmates, discuss the three main words
in the topic: *impact*, *technology*, and *workplace*. What words do you associate
with each of these key terms? Write them under the appropriate headings. An
example is given under each heading.

1. Impact

   improves things

   _____

   _____

   _____

2. Technology

computers

_____

_____

_____

3. Workplace

employees

_____

_____

_____

Exercise 8: Using Specific Language

The lists you created in Exercise 7 can be refined even more by adding specific words or phrases that help make each item clearer. For example, instead of discussing the general term *employees* in your paper, you might want to discuss the specific idea *employees' ability to earn a living.*

Add a word or phrase that makes each idea listed in Exercise 7 more specific. You can use the reading selections in Units Eight and Nine to help you find examples.

Exercise 9: Revising Your Preliminary Thesis

1. In the space below, write the preliminary thesis statement you developed at the end of Unit Eight.

_____

_____

2. Circle each of the main words in the statement of your thesis. Then make lists of the words you associate with these key terms, as you did in Exercise 7.

3. For each item, add a word or phrase that makes the item more specific, as you did in Exercise 8.

4. Revise your thesis statement, using some of the words or phrases you listed above to make your statement more specific. You may make changes in your preliminary thesis, or you may write an entirely new statement. Here is an example of the kind of thesis statement this process might produce:

> The development of the computer has had a profound impact on the workplace, changing the way many jobs are done. Therefore, I think training is the most important issue because it affects people's ability to get and keep jobs.

You will probably use only a few of the new words and phrases. Save the rest; they will be useful when you begin to develop your ideas in the first draft of your paper.

Exercise 10: Supporting General Statements

When you write your first draft, you will need to be even more specific than you have been in your thesis statement, adding information and examples to support your thesis. These examples and information explain or expand the general statements you make.

A. Below are some general statements from the reading material in this unit. Find the sentence or sentences in the reading material that explain or provide specific details about each general statement. Write the supporting sentences in the space provided. This time, use the author's exact words. The paragraph numbers in parentheses tell you where to look for the information in each reading selection.

1. From "The God That Limps," Unit Eight, page 128.

The spreading of microprocessors and computerized machinery threatens to carry this process even further in some applications, increasing the supervision of workers and further reducing their scope for independent thought and action. (paragraph 4)

_____

_____

2. From "Automation of America's Offices, 1985–2000," Unit Nine, page 145.

In the first stage of automation (large computers), the tendency was to make affected jobs more narrowly defined—in other words, to rationalize work. (paragraph 5)

_____

_____

_____

3. From "Automation of America's Offices, 1985–2000," Unit Nine, page 145. Many firms have decided that computer and communication technologies are often most effective in reducing costs when control, communication, and decision-making are decentralized and when hierarchic organization and functional specialization of tasks are reduced. (paragraph 6)

_____

_____

B. Make additional notes about any facts or examples in the reading selections in Units Eight and Nine that will support *your* thesis.

Look for main ideas and write them in your own words. Occasionally you might want to use the author's exact words to make a point. Copy these sentences accurately and put quotation marks around them, as you did in Unit Four. For each fact or example that you include in your notes, indicate the source, whether you have paraphrased the author or used the author's own words.

_____

_____

Writing the First Draft

CONTENT

Write the first draft of a term paper in which you discuss the following question:

> Technology has had a profound impact on the workplace. As you examine the way technological advances have affected workers and their environment, what do you think the most important issue is? Why do you think this issue is important?

Base your paper on the information and ideas in the reading selections in both Unit Eight and Unit Nine.

AUDIENCE

Your audience is your instructor and the other members of the class. As you write, however, keep in mind that this is the sort of paper that could be shared with groups of workers or employers who are considering changes in the workplace. Think about what kind of information would be useful for such a group.

PROCEDURE

- Begin your paper by stating the issues. Identify the issues by grouping together problems that are similar or related in some way. Make a general statement about each group of problems that tells how they are related. This discussion of the issues will be the introduction to your term paper. It will tell your audience what kind of impact technology has on the workplace.

- Weigh, or evaluate, the importance of the issues you have chosen to discuss. Think about the issues and use your judgment. Decide which issue matters the most. This is the one you will discuss in detail.

- State your position. Which issue is the most important? Why? Support your position with facts and examples from the reading material. You may not need to use all the reading material. Select what is most useful for you. If you want to, you can also use recent magazines or newspapers for additional information or draw examples from personal experience. Remember to summarize and combine information from different sources.

- Your first draft should be three to four double-spaced, typed pages or five to six double-spaced, handwritten pages.

UNIT TEN
WRITING A TERM PAPER

PART THREE: REVISING

Technology

In this unit, the final one of the three units that deal with writing a term paper, you will complete your paper by writing a second draft. To prepare, you will first do some revision activities that focus on the following points:

♦ writing an introduction for your paper

♦ writing a conclusion for your paper

♦ using direct and indirect quotations

There are no reading selections in this unit. Instead, you will be using the selections in Units Eight and Nine for many of the revision activities. You will also be rereading the first draft of your term paper and making changes in it.

THE SECOND DRAFT

Learning about Writing II

WRITING AN INTRODUCTION

Although it is the first thing in the paper, the introduction is often the last thing to be written. As long as you have a thesis statement, you have a way of getting started. Later on, the thesis statement can be expanded into an introduction that catches your reader's attention. There are many effective ways to introduce an essay or term paper. The following exercises will show you several, and you can choose the one that works best for your paper.

Exercise 1: Beginning with a Concept

A. Here are the first two paragraphs of "The Tyranny of the Clock." Reread them. Then discuss the following questions with your classmates.

In no characteristic is existing society in the West so sharply distinguished from the earlier societies, whether of Europe or the East, than in its conception of time. To the ancient Chinese or Greek, to the Arab herdsman or Mexican people of today, time is represented in the cyclical processes of nature, the alternation of day and night, the passage from season to season. The nomads and farmers measured and still measure their day from sunrise to sunset, and their year in term of the seedtime and harvest, of the falling leaf and the thawing ice. The farmer worked according to the elements; the craftsman for so long as he felt it necessary to perfect his product. . . .

Modern Western man, however, lives in a world which runs according to the mechanical and mathematical symbols of clock time. The clock dictates his movement and inhibits his actions. The clock turns time from a process of nature into a commodity that can be measured and bought and sold like soup or sultanas. . . .

1. Look at the notes you made for the first Writing Warm-up in Unit 8 (page 127). What is the main idea of the whole essay?

2. What is the main idea of these two paragraphs? Which sentence sums up that idea? Where is this sentence placed? Is this sentence the statement of Woodcock's main idea, or thesis, for the whole essay?

3. Look again at the entire selection (Unit Eight, pp. 125–126). What ideas in the rest of the essay are related to Woodcock's thesis?

Woodcock opens his essay by exploring the concept of time, which is one of the main ideas underlying the whole essay.

B. What are some of the concepts you could explore in an introduction to your paper? List some of the major concepts discussed in your paper.

_____

_____

_____

Exercise 2: Using a Generalization

A. Reread the first paragraph of the article "Automation of America's Offices, 1985–2000" that follows. Then discuss the questions with your classmates.

Office automation can substitute for labor, supplement labor, or reorganize work and thereby make labor more efficient. It can allow highly technical, knowledge-intensive work to be done by relatively untrained and unskilled, lower-paid workers. . . . It can change the characteristics and skills associated with occupations and alter their role and relative importance to an industry. It can allow office work to be done away from the office and outside of conventional office hours, even outside the country.

1. What is the main idea of this opening paragraph? Which sentence expresses it?

2. Look again at the entire selection (Unit Nine, pp. 145–148). What is the main idea or thesis?

3. Does the opening sentence express the entire thesis or part of the thesis?

4. How would you complete the first sentence if it ended this way?

   . . . and thereby make labor more efficient; however _____

_____

Does the rewritten sentence express the author's entire thesis?

This article opens with a generalization that is important to the author's thesis. The generalization is made in one sentence. You have worked with this kind of introduction in Unit Two (pages 29–30). There you developed generalizations based on how different cultures treated the concepts of time and interaction distance.

B. What are some of the generalizations about technology that you could use in an introduction to your paper? List them here.

_____

_____

Exercise 3: Using Examples

A. Read this excerpt from the article "How America Has Run Out of Time" by Nancy Gibbs. Then discuss the questions with your classmates.

In Florida a man bills his ophthalmologist $90 for keeping him waiting for an hour. In California a woman hires somebody to do her shopping for her—out of a catalog. Twenty bucks pays someone to pick up the dry cleaning, $250 to cater dinner for four, $1,500 will buy a fax machine for the car. "Time," concludes pollster Louis Harris, who has charted America's loss of it, "may have become the most precious commodity in the land."

1. What do you think the author's thesis for the entire article might be?

2. What is the main idea of this paragraph? What sentence sums up this idea? Considering the title of the article, does this sentence seem to express the author's thesis?

3. What is the function of the sentences that precede the last sentence? To get the effect, read the paragraph again, this time beginning with the last sentence. Which version is more interesting?

4. As you read the examples, did examples from your own experience come to mind? Were the author's choices interesting? Were they believable? Why or why not?

Gibbs uses examples drawn from a wide range of American life and activities to prepare the reader for the concluding generalization—that time is the most precious commodity in the land. Examples capture a reader's interest directly if they are believable and if they support the main idea of the essay.

B. **What examples could you use to introduce your thesis? (Remember that you can draw on personal experience or outside reading material for your term paper.) List your examples here.**

_____

_____

_____

WRITING A CONCLUSION

Beginning writers are often told to close their essays by restating the thesis. The following exercises will show you several different ways to add interest and information to the conclusion of your paper.

Exercise 4: Ending with a Question

A. **Read the following sentences from "Automation of America's Offices, 1985–2000." Then discuss the questions with your classmates.**

. . . Historically, the choice of full-time or part-time work has been regarded as the individual's prerogative. We must then ask: is this still a free choice, and will it be so in the future? To what extent is *involuntary* part-time work increasing?

1. Look again at the entire selection (Unit Nine, pp. 145–148). How are these questions related to the thesis? Are these questions answered in the text of the article?

2. What do you think the author's answers to these questions might be? How would you answer these questions? What else would you need to know to answer them?

3. Based on your reading and discussion, do you think these questions are logical extensions of the thesis?

This article closes with a series of questions that are related to but go beyond the original thesis. By asking questions not answered in the article itself, the author challenges the reader to supply his or her own answers. This kind of closing succeeds when the questions are not merely interesting or provocative but are logical extensions of the topic/thesis.

B. Write a question or questions you could use to end your your paper.

_____

_____

Exercise 5: Ending with a Recommendation

A. Read the ending of "The Tyranny of the Clock" and discuss the questions with your classmates. Notice that the author begins by restating the thesis; then he summarizes. What does he do next?

The problem of the clock is, in general, similar to that of the machine. Mechanical time is valuable as a means of coordination of activities in a highly developed society, just as the machine is valuable as a means of reducing unnecessary labor to a minimum. Both are valuable for the contribution they make to the smooth running of society and should be used insofar as they assist men to cooperate efficiently and to eliminate monotonous toil and social confusion. But neither should be allowed to dominate men's lives as they do today. Now the movement of the clock sets the tempo of men's lives—they become the servant of the concept of time which they themselves have made. . . . In a sane and free society . . . mechanical time should be relegated to its true function of a means of reference and coordination and men would return again to a balanced view of life no longer dominated by time regulation and the worship of the clock. . . .

1. How would Woodcock like to see modern life changed? What sentence tells you that?

2. Look again at the whole selection (Unit Eight, pp. 125–126). In light of the rest of the essay, does this suggestion surprise you? Why or why not?

3. What phrase tells you that Woodcock thinks his recommendation is an unlikely one?

4. What does Woodcock want the reader to do about his suggestion?

Making a recommendation that solves one of the problems mentioned in an essay is an effective closing—even when the author does not think his or her suggestion will be taken. Like the question strategy, the recommendation leaves the reader still thinking about the thesis and its implications.

B. Make notes about a recommendation you could use as the conclusion of your paper. Remember that an effective recommendation should be directly related to your thesis.

_____

_____

Exercise 6: Ending with a Quote

A. Read the ending of "The Growth of the Global Office" and discuss the questions with your classmates.

Cathy O'Grady, a 23-year-old native of Castleisland, finds the work more stimulating than her two previous jobs, as a part-time tour guide at an Irish heritage museum and teaching English in Spain. "Faraway hills are green," Ms. O'Grady said, "but I missed home. I like it here and now I have a job as well."

1. Look again at the whole article (Unit Nine, pp. 136–139). What is the author's thesis?

2. What does Ms. O'Grady mean? Explain the meaning of the quote in your own words.

3. How does the quote support the main idea of the article?

4. What does the quote add to the article that wasn't there before?

Steve Lohr uses a quote to add a human interest touch to his article on the global office. A quote can be an effective conclusion when it adds something or when it restates the thesis.

B. Look at the conclusion in the draft of your paper. Could it use a quote? Review all the documents you have used and write one or two quotes that might be suitable.

_____

_____

Exercise 7: Revising Your Introduction and Conclusion

Review the notes you made for Exercises 1 through 6. Choose a method for writing an introduction and conclusion that you like and that you think works the best for your paper. Then rewrite the introduction and conclusion of your paper.

USING THE WORDS OF AN EXPERT TO SUPPORT YOUR POSITION

An effective way to support your position is to use the words of an expert, in either a direct or an indirect quotation. You can use what someone has said in an interview or what someone has written in an article or book. Here are some of the things you can do with a direct or indirect quotation:

- Emphasize something you have said
- Lend authority and credibility to what you have said
- Give additional information
- Supply an explanation or a commentary
- Introduce a new topic

Remember that a direct quotation repeats the writer's or speaker's exact words and is enclosed in a set of quotation marks. An indirect quotation paraphrases what the writer or speaker said, and there are no quotation marks around it. A direct quotation is a good choice when the writer's or speaker's words are special, and you do not want to change them. An indirect quotation is better when the idea matters more than the exact words. Whether you use a direct or an indirect quotation, you must cite your source—that is, tell whose words or ideas you are using.

Exercise 8: Using a Direct Quotation for Support

A. Read the following paragraphs from "Calling Collect? A Computer Is at Your Service." Then discuss the questions with your classmates.

The savings will be only for the companies; calling rates are not expected to fall.

"This was bound to happen sooner or later because it's just too expensive for phone companies to keep completing these types of calls with human operators," said John Reddy, a business professor at the Wilkes-Barre campus of Pennsylvania State University.

1. What is the purpose of the quotation?

2. Which words are John Reddy's? Are they being quoted directly? How is this shown?

3. How does the writer identify the person being quoted?

4. Find a place in your paper where you could use a direct quotation effectively for the same purpose. Make an X where the quotation could be added and write the word *quote* in the margin.

B. Read the following paragraphs from "The Growth of the Global Office." Then discuss the questions with your classmates.

But the forces pushing corporations to send white-collar work abroad go well beyond the wage benefits, as shown by the New York Life case. With unemployment low, especially in the New York region, the company found that recruiting workers for low-level jobs like claims processing became more and more difficult. Moreover, employee turnover in claims offices in the industry is high, as much as 30 percent a year. And changing demographic trends will aggravate the problem. In the decade ending in 1995, the number of 18- to 24-year-olds in the American work force will decline by 17.5 percent.

"The demographics make this a nationwide challenge," said John Foy, a vice president of New York Life. "American companies will find it much more difficult to find skilled workers at home for the rest of this century."

1. What is the purpose of the quotation?

2. Who is being quoted? How is the speaker identified?

3. Are the speaker's exact words given? How is this shown?

4. Find a place in your paper where you could use a direct quotation effectively for the same purpose. Make an X where the quotation could be added and write the word *quote* in the margin.

C. Read the following paragraph from "Calling Collect? A Computer Is at your Service." Then discuss the questions with your classmates.

Mr. Reddy, who spent 25 years as a strategic planner in operator services with the old Bell system, predicted that electronic operators would "eventually replace about half of the estimated 70,000 operators employed by local and long-distance phone companies across the nation."

1. What is the purpose of the quotation?

2. Where does the quotation begin? How is this shown?

3. How is the speaker identified?

4. Find a place in your paper where you could use a direct quotation effectively for the same purpose. Make an X where the quotation could be added and write the word *quote* in the margin.

Exercise 9: Using Indirect Quotations for Support

A. Read the following excerpt from "The Tyranny of the Clock." Then discuss the questions with your classmates.

The clock, as Lewis Mumford points out, represents the key machine of the machine age, both for its influence on technics and for its influence on the habits of men. Technically, the clock was the first really automatic machine that attained any importance in the lives of men. Prior to its invention, the common machines were of such a nature that their operation depended on some external and unreliable force such as human or animal muscle, water or wind.

1. Which idea in this paragraph is Lewis Mumford's? How does George Woodcock tell us that he is paraphrasing Mumford's idea?

2. Why do you think Woodcock uses this indirect quotation here?

3. Find a place in your paper where you could use an indirect quotation effectively the way Woodcock has. Make an X where the quotation could be added and write the word *quote* in the margin.

B. Read the following excerpt from "The Growth of the Global Office." Then discuss the questions with your classmates.

Travelers opened its software development office in July 1987. It now has a staff of 27, nearly all of them young Irish computer scientists. The office has performed well, said Peter C. Noonan, managing director of Travelers of Ireland, Ltd., but he has noticed that attitudes toward sending software chores to Ireland vary considerably from department to department in Hartford.

1. Which part of this paragraph contains Peter C. Noonan's words?

2. Are his exact words given? How do you know?

3. What do these words of Peter Noonan's add to the paragraph?

4. Find a place in your paper where you could use an indirect quotation effectively the way Lohr has. Make an X where the quotation could be added and write the word *quote* in the margin.

C. Read the following excerpt from "Calling Collect? A Computer Is at Your Service." Then discuss the questions with your classmates.

The telephone companies contend that the systems will greatly reduce the need for human operators and the cost of completing calls at a time when the number of collect and third-party calls is increasing. But union leaders say the new technology will provide an excuse for layoffs, and others question the quality of service provided by electronic operators.

1. The information in this paragraph comes from three different sources. What are they?

2. How does the writer show what each source said?

3. What is the purpose of this paragraph?

4. Find a place in your paper where you could use an indirect quotation effectively for the same purpose. Make an X where the quotation could be added and write the word *quote* in the margin.

Exercise 10: Writing Direct Quotations Correctly

Look at these examples of direct quotations from the selections in Unit Nine. Then discuss the questions with your classmates.

Example A: "As I looked at it closely, it seemed that we would be foolish not to try going to Ireland," Mr. Foy said.

Example B: "You've got to earn the credibility within the company," Mr. Noonan said. "Here, you're not just a little removed from headquarters. You're in Ireland."

Example C: "Faraway hills are green," Ms. O'Grady said, "but I missed home. I like it here and now I have a job as well."

1. How many sentences of Mr. Foy's are quoted in Example A? Where has the writer placed the words *Mr. Foy said*? What punctuation marks has the writer used at the end of the quotation? What punctuation mark has the writer used after the word *said*?

2. How many sentences of Mr. Noonan's are quoted in Example B? Where has the writer placed the words *Mr. Noonan said*? How many sets of quotation marks has the writer used? Where are they placed?

3. How many sentences of Ms. O'Grady's are quoted in Example C? Where has the writer placed the words *Ms. O'Grady said*? What punctuation marks has the writer used after the word *said*? Why does the word *but* begin with a lower case *b*?

Exercise 11: Punctuating Direct Quotations

Add quotation marks to the direct quotations below.

These quotations are taken from the reading selections in Unit Nine. When you have finished the exercise, check whether you punctuated the quotation correctly.

1. We are introducing this new service to keep our costs for operator services under control, said Phil Jones, a spokesman for Michigan Bell. It will allow us to continue processing these calls at no extra increase to consumers. (Page 142, "Calling Collect," paragraph 18.)

2. Consumers always have the option of switching to a live operator if they are feeling lazy or need special assistance, Mr. Lloyd said. (Page 142, "Calling Collect," paragraph 23.)

3. At the American Telephone and Telegraph Company, Jim Selzer, vice president of operator services, said: Operators are a value-added service and we use them as differentiators. If we introduced electronic operators for these calls, many of our customers would see it as a slight and would be more inclined to use our competitors. (Page 143, "Calling Collect," paragraph 26.)

Exercise 12: Adding Support to Your Paper

A. **Reread the first draft of your term paper and ask yourself the following questions:**

- Where, in addition to the places you have already identified, can you strengthen your position by using the words of an expert, quoted directly?

- Where else can you add ideas or information in an indirect quotation?

- Can a direct or indirect quotation be used effectively in the introduction or the conclusion?

B. **Look again at the reading selections in Units Eight and Nine and at any other reading you may have done for your term paper. Identify material that you can either quote directly or paraphrase for an indirect quotation. To avoid over-quoting, make sure the material you choose is relevant and will serve a real purpose in your paper.**

C. **Make an X on your first draft at the spot where you plan to add each direct or indirect quotation. For the indirect quotations, write out the paraphrase on a separate sheet of paper. Remember to cite your source. For the direct quotations, copy exactly the words you intend to use. (You can quote part of a sentence, a whole sentence, or more than one sentence.) Put quotation marks around the quoted material and cite the source. You can use the examples on page 164 as models for punctuating your quotations.**

WRITING A BIBLIOGRAPHY

The final step in citing your sources is to write a list of all the books and articles you have used. For books the list includes the title, the author, the publisher, and the date. For magazine and newspaper articles it includes the title, the author, the name of the magazine or newspaper, the date, and the pages used.

The bibliography below cites the sources used in Units 8 through 10. Before you write your own bibliography, check with your instructor. Your instructor may prefer a different form.

Gibbs, Nancy. "How America Has Run Out of Time." *Time* 24 April, 1989: 58.

Lohr, Steve. "The Growth of the Global Office." *New York Times* 18 October 1988, sec. D:1.

Norman, Colin. *The God That Limps.* New York: Norton, 1981.

Sims, Calvin. "Calling Collect? A Computer Is at Your Service." *New York Times* 12 June 1989, sec. A:1.

U.S. Congress. Office of Technological Assessment. *Automation of America's Offices, 1985–2000.* Washington: GPO, OTA-C17-287, Dec. 1985.

Woodcock, George. "The Tyranny of the Clock." *Work and Society.* Ed. Social Science Faculty, La Guardia Community College. Dubuque, Iowa: Kendall/Hunt Pub. Co., 1979.

Exercise 13: *Writing a Bibliography for Your Paper*

On an index card, list each book or article you used while writing your term paper.

You must give credit to all your sources — the ones from which you have quoted directly and the ones that have supplied you with general information and ideas. Arrange the cards so that the last names of the authors are in alphabetical order. If there is no author, use the name of the group or institution responsible for the publication. Then write the bibliography, following either the format shown above or the format your teacher recommends. In the final draft, the bibliography should follow the last page of your term paper.

Writing the Second Draft

Now that you have had a chance to think about what you have written and to make a few changes, you are ready to write the second draft of your term paper. Read the first draft again. Ask yourself the following questions or work with a partner to answer these questions about each other's draft:

- Is there a clear thesis statement? Does it express your position?
- Is the main idea of each paragraph clear? Do the details support the main idea? Do the details strengthen your position?
- Are the relationships between the body paragraphs and the thesis clear?
- Are the ideas connected in a clear, logical way?
- Are the relationships between ideas in the paragraphs clear?
- Are direct and indirect quotations used appropriately?
- Are the sources cited for all direct and indirect quotations?
- Are indirect quotations paraphrased correctly?
- Are direct quotations punctuated correctly?

- Is there an effective introduction?
- Is there an effective closing?
- Does your bibliography follow the recommended format? Does it include all your sources?
- Does your paper reflect an understanding of the writing process presented throughout this book?

Make whatever changes are necessary to make your thesis clear, unify your essay, and strengthen your position.

Writing the Final Copy

When you are finished revising, edit your essay for errors in spelling, grammar, and punctuation. If you have not already given your essay a title, add one now. Copy your revised draft neatly on clean paper before you hand it in.